HOW COLLEGES EVALUATE PROFESSORS

CURRENT POLICIES AND PRACTICES IN EVALUATING CLASSROOM TEACHING PERFORMANCE IN LIBERAL ARTS COLLEGES

PETER SELDIN, PH.D.

Library of Congress Catalog Card Number: 75-6190

First Printing, April 1975
Second Printing, August 1975
Third Printing, February 1976
Fourth Printing, November 1976

BLYTHE-PENNINGTON, LTD.

Croton - on - Hudson, New York 10520

Printed in The United States of America

CONTENTS

378
.122
S449h

LIST OF TABLES

Table

PREFACE

Faculty evaluation is an important and sensitive problem. Nearly everyone in higher education, faculty and administrators alike, is concerned with it. Yet, for the most part, faculty evaluation is whispered and gossiped about but it is seldom confronted directly.

This research study was developed with an eye toward bringing into the open, the specifics of just how colleges today cope, as they must, with necessary evaluation of both overall and teaching performance of members of their faculty.

Special mention is due Dr. Lillian Restaino, Associate Professor of Education, who gave unstintingly of herself while serving as mentor for this Fordham University doctoral dissertation.

While it is true that she served as proofreader, my wife, Pat, should especially be thanked because she has borne, with customary good humor and spirit, the brunt of my time-consuming wrestling match with this research study.

I

INTRODUCTION

Every academic year, the teaching performances of thousands of liberal arts college faculty members are reviewed and evaluated. On the basis of these evaluations, important decisions are made concerning the status of those subject to review. At each institution, some faculty members may be granted promotion in rank while others are denied such promotion. Some faculty members may be granted substantial salary increments while others are given more modest salary increments. The contracts of some staff members may be renewed while the contracts of others within the same institution and department are terminated.

Since these personnel decisions affect the future of academic institutions as well as thousands of faculty members, it seems proper to raise the following fundamental question: How adequate and equitable are the policies and procedures that served to justify the decisions concerning academic personnel?

There is some reason to believe that the policies and procedures leave a great deal to be desired as far as objectivity, consistency, and predictability are concerned. This is the opinion of many faculty members and administrators who have been sharply critical, in recent years, of the practices used to evaluate the level of teaching performance of college professors.

This research study has been undertaken in order to determine whether such strong criticism of current faculty appraisal techniques is justified. It is hoped that the beginnings of an empirical base for the critical appraisal of current policies and practices will result from the research reported here.

A nationwide investigation in this area has not taken place since the Astin and Lee study in 1966, several years prior to the eruption of substantial campus pressures that may have contributed to revision of college policies and practices. The results of this investigation will provide an opportunity to measure changes that have occurred in the seven years since the previous study was undertaken.

7

THE PROBLEM

Statement of the problem. There were two aspects to the problem under investigation. First, the study sought to determine the current policies and practices used in liberal arts colleges to evaluate classroom teaching performance of members of the faculty, and second, the study sought to determine the manner in which such evaluation was used in making decisions regarding retention, salary increment, and promotion in rank.

The sub-problems related to evaluation of teaching performance were as follows:

1. To what extent was quality of teaching performance considered a major factor in evaluation of overall faculty performance in liberal arts colleges?

2. From what specific sources is information obtained in liberal arts colleges for use in the evaluation of the teaching performance of individual members of the faculty?

3. To what extent were rating forms or other instruments employed to gather information on the quality of teaching performance of individual members of the faculty in liberal arts colleges?

4. To what extent have changes occurred in the policies and practices used in liberal arts colleges to evaluate the classroom teaching performance of faculty members since the survey by Astin and Lee (1966)?

5. What were the personal opinions of the academic deans about methods of evaluating faculty teaching performance that relied primarily on students, faculty colleagues, or faculty self-evaluation as sources of information for the evaluation of a faculty member's teaching performance?

6. To what degree did the academic deans express satisfaction with the policies and practices used in their colleges to evaluate the classroom teaching performance of faculty members?

7. To what degree were written criteria used to measure and evaluate the teaching performance in decisions of promotion in rank and contract renewal?

8. Which behavioral criteria were rated most important in evaluating faculty teaching performance in decisions of promotion in rank and contract renewal?

9. To what extent did the policies and practices used to evaluate faculty teaching performance for the purpose of contract renewal differ from the policies and practices used to evaluate faculty teaching performance for the purpose of promotion in rank?

8

DEFINITION OF TERMS

Terms used in this study were defined as follows:

Academic Dean. The term academic dean refers to the administrator within each liberal arts college who normally has major responsibility for academic decisions (as opposed to responsibility in the areas of student personnel, physical plant, fund-raising, athletics, etc.) and who is recorded as the academic dean in the Education Directory (1971), published by the United States Office of Education, Washington, D.C.

Contract Renewal. For purposes of this study, the term "contract renewal" is defined as the reappointment of a faculty member to a full-time teaching position. The effective date of a contract renewal is normally September 1 of the academic year immediately following expiration of the faculty member's previous teaching appointment at the same institution of higher education.

Evaluation of Teaching Performance. The definition of evaluation of teaching performance used by Astin and Lee (1966) has been adopted for purposes of this study. The term designates the appraisal process of exercising discretion and judgment with regard to determining the level of pedagogical effectiveness of a full-time member of the teaching faculty.

Faculty Member. In this study, the term faculty member refers to a full-time member of the teaching faculty of a liberal arts college. Such faculty members have responsibility for the education of college students enrolled in their courses.

Liberal Arts College. The term liberal arts college refers, in this study, to an accredited four year, private institution of higher education in the United States which is not part of a university and is designated as a liberal arts college by the United States Office of Education in its Education Directory (1971).

Overall Faculty Evaluation. For the purposes of this study, the definition of overall faculty evaluation used by Cook and Neville (1971) has been adopted. The term designates the composite appraisal of a faculty member's performance in several different areas including, for example, teaching, advising, college services, and publication. Further, overall faculty evaluation includes the act of weighting the measured data obtained about a teacher by superimposing a set of values on to the data.

Promotion in Rank. The term promotion in rank refers to faculty advancement in position from the level of instructor to assistant professor, assistant professor to associate professor, or associate professor to professor. Applications for advancement in professorial level are evaluated in accordance with specific qualifications that generally are enumerated as part of the

9

faculty statutes of a liberal arts college.

Systematic Student Evaluation. As defined in this study, essential elements of systematic student evaluation include carefully designated and statistically validated questionnaires as well as a consistent procedure for obtaining the subjective opinions of students regarding the teaching effectiveness of their classroom instructor (Balyeat, 1971).

Teaching Behaviors. This term designates specific, observable pedagogical characteristics and traits that are frequently associated with instructional practices of faculty members who are considered to be effective teachers. The presence or absence of these pedagogical behaviors is often used to evaluate the teaching performance of faculty members for purposes of contract renewal or promotion in rank.

Teaching Performance. In this study, the term teaching performance refers to the instructional effectiveness of full-time members of the faculty who are teaching regularly scheduled classes which are offered to college students for academic credit.

SIGNIFICANCE OF THE STUDY

More than thirty years ago Logan Wilson, President of the University of Texas, wrote in The Academic Man (1942):

Indeed, it is no exaggeration to say that the most critical problem confronted in the social organization of any (college or) university is the proper evaluation of faculty services, and giving due recognition through the impartial assignment of status (p. 112).

In spite of the intervening years, it appears that a substantial number of colleges and universities have not yet adequately dealt with the issue of developing proper evaluation of faculty services. More specifically, those institutions apparently have not yet developed the policies and practices that are necessary to evaluate faculty teaching performance meaningfully and equitably.

Classroom teaching is the reason for existence of the majority of colleges. Private liberal arts colleges, particularly, have traditionally emphasized quality classroom teaching. Academic deans in liberal arts colleges identified classroom teaching as the most important factor in the evaluation of faculty performance in the study by Gustad (1961) and the followup investigation conducted by Astin and Lee (1966).

Apparently, in the world of higher education, informal nonsystematic evaluation of faculty teaching performance goes on continuously. Students assess what they regard as the teacher's effectiveness and pass their appraisals on to other students. Faculty colleagues, department chairmen, and deans gain impressions of teaching performance often based on unsystematically collected information.

Unfortunately, data gathered through such a diffused approach to evaluating teaching performance frequently forms the basis upon which faculty personnel decisions are made.

Although classroom teaching has been recognized as being of critical importance, the methods by which it is evaluated have been sharply criticized by academic researchers.

Hodgkinson (1971), Center for Research and Development in Higher Education, University of California, Berkeley, stated his view of the criteria frequently used to evaluate teaching performance: "It is quite easy to document a large number of cases...in which the evaluative criteria are whimsical and have little to do with the teacher's performance" (p. 49).

The system used in a substantial number of colleges to evaluate the teaching performance of faculty members was summarized by Eble (1972) in this manner: "It stresses...secrecy rather than openness, and the informal, inferential, and subjective judgment of teaching rather than the systematic, first hand, and objective" (p. 64).

In 1966 Astin and Lee investigated, for the American Council on Education, the policies and practices employed by colleges to evaluate faculty teaching performance for the purpose of reaching faculty personnel decisions. The responses of 1110 academic deans from colleges and universities differing in size, selectivity and geographic location, led the authors to conclude that many institutions "suffer from an inability to evaluate classroom effectiveness" (p. 307). Astin and Lee asserted that meaningful evaluation of the teaching performance of faculty members was only rarely found since the methods employed to assess teaching effectiveness were frequently inaccurate and unreliable.

Since 1966, however, colleges have responded to different kinds of substantial pressures. Student activism on campus, for example, has resulted in a sharply expanded role in academic governance and decision-making for the student body. In addition, the higher rate of young Ph.D.'s entering the teaching profession may have persuaded colleges to adopt more accurate methods of evaluating the teaching performance of these younger members of the faculty in order that more appropriate decisions might be made about retention and promotion.

Finally, worsening economic conditions have forced many colleges to adopt cost-effectiveness programs. An important part of the resulting accountability would seem to be the need to develop more formalized and systematic methods of evaluating faculty performance.

As a result of the pressure on liberal arts colleges to modify some of their pre-1966 traditional methods of operation, the methods previously used to evaluate teaching performance may have been revised. A national study to confirm this, however, has not yet been carried out.

It is expected that this investigation will provide substantial information in the following important areas:

1. The level of change in the practices of evaluating teaching performance since the 1966 study by Astin and Lee.

2. The opinions of academic deans regarding approaches to teacher evaluation that rely primarily on either students, department colleagues, or faculty self-evaluation.

3. The similarities and differences between teaching behaviors used in evaluating instructional performance for the purpose of contract renewal and for the purpose of promotion in rank.

4. The level of satisfaction expressed by academic deans in liberal arts colleges with the policies and practices used in their college to evaluate faculty teaching performance.

5. The estimation of academic deans of the level of satisfaction of most of their faculty with the policies and practices used in their college to evaluate faculty teaching performance.

ASSUMPTIONS OF THE STUDY

The following assumptions were made in this research study:

1. Some type of evaluation of faculty teaching performance existed in every liberal arts college.

2. Faculty teaching performance was considered in academic personnel decisions.

3. The academic dean was familiar with the policies and practices used in his college to evaluate faculty teaching performance.

4. The samples of liberal arts colleges obtained in the Astin and Lee (1966) study and the present research study are sufficiently similar for comparison of results.

LIMITATIONS OF THE STUDY

1. This research study was concerned only with the evaluation of teaching performance for the purpose of academic personnel

decision. It was not concerned with evaluation of teaching performance for the purpose of improvement of instruction.

2. This study was concerned only with the evaluation of teaching performance of members of the faculty who teach full-time on the undergraduate level in an accredited liberal arts college.

3. In order to limit the study so that the investigator, acting alone, could adequately carry out the research, only private liberal arts colleges, not part of a university and listed in the United States Office of Education, Education Directory (1971), were included in the population of this study.

4. While other academic administrators might have been able to respond, only academic deans were asked to indicate the policies and practices used in evaluating teaching performance in their college.

5. Faculty salary schedules and related faculty-union contract matters were not examined in this research study.

6. Since Part One of this study was a replication of segments of the 1966 study by Astin and Lee for the American Council on Education, it is subject to any limitations inherent in that study.

II

REVIEW OF RELEVANT RESEARCH

AND LITERATURE

In this chapter, research and literature on the evaluation of teaching effectiveness in higher education are reviewed in two parts: (1) importance and status of the evaluation of teaching performance, and (2) methods used to evaluate teaching effectiveness. A brief summary of the findings concludes the chapter.

RESEARCH AND LITERATURE RELATED TO THE
IMPORTANCE AND STATUS OF THE
EVALUATION OF TEACHING PERFORMANCE

Recent position papers and studies have demonstrated that the evaluation of teaching performance plays a central role in the appraisal of overall performance of faculty members on the undergraduate level.

Among several important reasons offered in a position paper by Gage (1959) for evaluating teaching is the traditional need for providing a broad base for administrative decisions on promotions, salaries and tenure.

Cartter (1967) stated that, in his view, the evaluation of teaching performance was of critical importance if professorial talent and resources were to be used with maximum effectiveness by an academic institution. He suggested that knowledge of the particular teaching strengths and weaknesses of individual members of the faculty was essential if a college or university was to develop a reputation for teaching excellence.

In the opinion of Howe (1967), a reputation for quality teaching is unlikely to develop until colleges and universities recognize the singular importance of teaching. This can only be done, according to Howe, by building an appraisal of teaching ability into existing systems for promotion and contract renewal.

A similar position was adopted by Wilson (1967). Noting the importance of effective teaching, particularly on an undergraduate level, he urged the adoption of a revised faculty appraisal system in which teaching would be evaluated, criticized, and

14

rewarded with the same degree of rigorous analysis that is now applied to a faculty member's research and publications. If that were done, according to Wilson, the true importance of effective teaching would be more clearly recognized.

Recent studies also have underscored the importance accorded by many educators to the evaluation of teaching performance.

Results of the nationwide study of faculty evaluation systems conducted by Gustad (1961) using 584 colleges and universities of different sizes and selectivity, indicated that classroom teaching was the most important factor in evaluation. It was ranked number one in importance by the deans of liberal arts colleges as well as by the deans of private universities, state universities, state colleges, teachers colleges and professional and technical colleges.

Byrnes and Jamrich (1962) found that outstanding teaching served as the sole criterion for promotion in rank in 52 percent of the 310 participating institutions of the American Association of Colleges for Teacher Education. Approximately 87 percent indicated that salary increases were made on the basis of level of teaching performance.

In a follow-up of the Gustad study conducted for the American Council on Education, Astin and Lee (1966) reported that 97.6 percent of the academic deans in 1110 colleges and universities indicated that classroom teaching was a "major factor" in the evaluation of faculty for promotion, salary increase or tenure.

In his doctoral dissertation, Goforth (1966) investigated the desirable characteristics of college teachers as perceived by presidents and deans of liberal arts colleges. The author used a random sample of one-third of all accredited, undergraduate, coeducational, liberal arts colleges. Among his major findings was the very high rank given to teaching and related activities as a major qualification for promotion. Moreover, Goforth found that five of the ten more desirable characteristics were concerned with pedagogy.

Most faculty members appear to agree with the importance accorded teaching evaluation. This has been underscored by Gaff and Wilson (1970) in a study commissioned by the American Association of University Professors and the Association of American Colleges. Canvassing 1050 faculty members at six selected colleges and universities that differed in size, selectivity and geographical location, the authors found that:

> 85 percent of the faculty respondents endorsed the idea that a formal program of teacher evaluation should be used by the college in making academic decisions about

such matters as salary, promotion and tenure (p. 29).

In addition, Gaff and Wilson reported that 92 percent of the 1050 faculty members believed that teaching effectiveness should be "very important" in promotion decisions.

Balyeat (1971) randomly sampled approximately 3000 faculty members, Ph.D. candidates and administrators in representative state and private institutions in all geographical areas of the United States. Reporting on the results of his study, sponsored by the Office of Education, Department of Health, Education and Welfare, Balyeat concluded that the single factor which "all hierarchical levels (from instructor to university president) considered the most important criterion for merit increases and promotion in rank was teaching effectiveness" (p. 5). Balyeat also found that administrators and faculty were in agreement that "teaching effectiveness should be recognized as the single most important contribution to the long-range goals and objectives of their institutions" (p. 3).

Swanson and Weaver (1972) found in their survey of faculty appraisal systems at 51 diverse colleges of Business Administration that without exception all of the respondents indicated that they included teaching performance in their appraisal of faculty. The single most frequently mentioned element in the appraisal of faculty performance was teaching ability.

Kenneth Eble (1972) visited 70 colleges and universities in 40 states including public and private, as well as rural and urban, institutions. He reported his conclusions following a two-year nationwide investigation into the evaluation of college teaching, sponsored by the American Association of University Professors and the Association of American Colleges, and funded by the Carnegie Corporation. Eble stated that:

> Amid the imperfect means now being used to judge a professor's competence, responsible judgments of teaching seem to offer more exact data than do other parts of the process (p. 30).

What clearly emerges from the above studies is the widely held belief that teaching performance is vital in the evaluation of college teachers. Because so great a weight is placed upon evaluation of teaching performance in the determination of teacher competency, experts in the area have expressed some concern with the accuracy and validity of the sources of these evaluations.

The current status of the evaluation of teaching performance has been the focus of several recent position papers.

Clark (1961) stated his belief that evaluation of teaching performance was often based on limited evidence. Moreover, he suggested that information collected in a generally haphazard and chaotic way frequently served as the basis for retention and promotion decisions.

Cohen and Brawer (1969) agreed with Clark and summarized their view as follows: "The best that can be said for current methods of evaluating faculty in institutions of higher education is that they are ineffectual and little regarded" (p. 63).

Blackburn (1970) described the situation with regard to evaluation of teaching performance as one where confusion reigns and faculty complain with justification. He urged that the serious study of the variables involved in faculty evaluation be given the highest priority.

Other educators in higher education have reached similar conclusions. Hodgkinson (1971), of the Center for Research and Development in Higher Education, at the University of California at Berkeley, described the criteria used to evaluate teaching performance in a large number of cases as "whimsical" and as having "little to do with the teacher's performance" (p. 49).

Similar conclusions have been reached in recent studies investigating the status of the evaluation of teaching performance in higher education.

In 1961, after completing a nationwide survey for the American Council on Education of 584 institutions, including liberal arts colleges, state colleges, private and state universities, John Gustad asserted:

It was not assumed, when this study was planned, that the situation with respect to faculty evaluation would be found to be good. What was somehow surprising, was the extent and depth of the chaos...factors are evaluated on a hit or miss basis (p. 210).

Little if any progress had occurred when Gustad (1967) commented on the results of a followup study of 1110 academic deans in colleges and universities by Astin and Lee investigating the policies and practices employed in higher education to evaluate faculty performance six years after his original investigation:

The almost imperceptible progress (in the area of evaluation of faculty teaching performance) is eloquent testimony

17

to the academic profession's unwillingness or inability, or both, to do what is needed to develop adequate and equitable methods for faculty evaluation (p. 265).

In his two-year investigation of the current status of the evaluation of teaching performance, Kenneth Eble (1972) appraised the situation in a random sample of 70 colleges and universities that varied in size, selectivity and geographic location. He concluded from his findings:

Much of the basis for judging teaching performance is largely inferential. Judgments are based on appraisals of a colleague's qualities of mind, manner of address, casual conversations with students and other colleagues, research and publications. Some of these may have a bearing upon teaching performance; some may not (p. 99).

In summary, it would appear that despite the singular importance accorded the evaluation of teaching performance in recent position papers and studies, the basis for judgment and the information that is gathered is of highly questionable value.

RESEARCH AND LITERATURE RELATED TO
METHODS OF EVALUATING TEACHING

Although a wide range of methods of teaching evaluation have been proposed in recent years, it would appear that most proposals rely heavily on self-evaluation, colleague evaluation or student evaluation as sources of information on teaching performance. In some cases a composite approach is used.

Self-Evaluation

A small number of educators have issued position papers proposing self-evaluation as an important element in the evaluation of teaching performance of faculty members. Simpson and Seidman (1962) generally supported self-evaluation although they reported to the American Association of Colleges of Teacher Education that lack of knowledge about the process of self-evaluation lessened its practical value.

Mayhew (1967) and Rovin (1967) both favored the use of self-evaluation, though each author cautioned against the use of self-evaluation, by itself, to justify salary or academic rank advances.

Further support for self-evaluation as a teaching appraisal technique came from Miller (1972). Although he cautioned that the majority of faculty members would need assistance in using self-evaluation constructively, Miller recommended that it be adopted as part of an evaluation system because:

> As one develops greater self-awareness, he is able to respond more effectively to the areas and interests of others, and he is more likely to observe unspoken clues to behaviors and needs (p. 35).

Moreover, Miller saw value in self-appraisal not only at the conclusion of a term but also in early-term evaluation designed to assist the professor in improving the course for the rest of the term.

There are several strong critics of the evaluation of teaching performance through self-evaluation. The criticism in their position papers has frequently been based on a mistrust of the accuracy and reliability of self-evaluation as a meaningful measuring device.

Bayley (1967) suggested that, in his opinion, although most college teachers believe they are capable of criticizing their own teaching performance, few actually do it. Bayley expressed little faith in the reliability of self-evaluation: "They (faculty) seem to believe that no one but themselves can recognize the worth of what an individual teacher is doing. That this attitude is an invitation to self-delusion hardly needs elaboration.... The word of each teacher can hardly be accepted at face value" (pp. 115-116).

A similar view was expressed by Ozmon (1967). He concluded a statement of his beliefs by asserting that self- evaluation of teaching performance was basically a faulty appraisal technique. Ozmon suggested that teachers in large numbers would say that they believed themselves to be good teachers and that honest self-evaluation would only rarely take place.

Eble (1972) concurred and pointed out that administrators, in particular, hesitate to place too much reliance on self-observations. He also suggested that the subjective nature of self-evaluation would not be a substantial addition to evaluation processes which, in his opinion, were most in need of objective data.

While not specifically criticizing self-evaluation, examination of the systems and models developed by a number of authors for the evaluation of teaching reveals that they have omitted self-evaluation from their systems. Among these authors are Morton (1961), Smart (1965), Brown (1967), Dressel (1967), Megaw (1967), Hunter (1969), Karman (1969), Hildebrand and Wilson (1970), and Cook and Neville (1971).

19

In summary, although self-evaluation of teaching performance is supported by a small number of researchers, other researchers have been sharply critical. Similarly, those who are designing models for evaluating teaching performance have not included it among their components.

Colleague Evaluation Through Classroom Visits

Colleague evaluation as a means of evaluation of teaching effectiveness is an approach that has frequently been suggested in the literature.

Morton (1961) urged the adoption of colleague evaluation through classroom observation. "This method (colleague evaluation) can be effectively used...when (the visit) involves friendliness and interest as well as a critical and instructual purpose" (p. 122). In his view, the observer must be supplied in advance with course outline or material to be covered as well as procedures to be used.

In a position paper, Smart (1965) suggested that faculty colleagues were in a singularly good position to judge the pedagogical wisdom employed in the classroom by a member of the faculty. For that reason, Smart urged that evaluation of teaching performance be based, in large measure, on colleague evaluation.

Bayley (1967), too, saw merit in colleague evaluation. He suggested several purposes that would be served by having faculty colleagues enter one another's classes:

> First, colleagues will provide as trustworthy critics of classroom activity and course organization as can be found. They will provide teachers with the essential element of feedback....Second, colleague observation...will provide the best information possible for the rewarding of superior teaching, and the discipline of inadequate teaching (pp. 116 - 117).

Examination of course outlines and material prior to classroom visitation was urged in a position paper by Bryant (1967). He favored the use of peer evaluation and expressed it in this manner:

> ...let us affirm the principle that the accused is entitled to a trial by a jury of his peers....A department chairman or his delegate, visiting a classroom, examining course materials, and discussing course objectives and techniques with the professor, will arrive at a more reliable evaluation

of a teacher's effectiveness than will an undergraduate who has his personal axe to grind (p. 329).

Classroom visitation as a means of gathering data for evaluation of teaching performance was also supported by Megaw (1967). He suggested the designation of a special committee of instruction consisting of elected faculty members each of whom would make visits to classrooms and submit reports on teaching effectiveness. Megaw also urged that the college or university financially support the committee of instruction by making an investment of up to three percent of total faculty costs.

The Committee on Undergraduate Teaching of the Hazen Foundation (1970) suggested in a position paper that classroom visitation could be useful in the evaluation of teaching performance and recommended its use. The Committee cautioned, however, that the proper academic atmosphere was necessary for it to succeed. While recognizing that classroom visitation was not widely practiced, the Committee suggested adoption of the Harvard model in which younger and older faculty members work together to discuss and evaluate each other's teaching performance.

Colleague evaluation of teaching performance was also endorsed by Gaff and Wilson (1971). In their position paper, the authors pointed out that by working together, faculty members can:

> ...establish priorities by encouraging certain kinds of behavior and discouraging other kinds. Colleagues can provide information and criticism...(and) can reinforce a teacher for his efforts and accomplishments. Since faculty members serve on review committees, they can recommend promotion or tenure...(p. 46).

Hodgkinson (1971) suggested that in his opinion, while colleague evaluation is subject to human frailty, it provides substantive data for clinical and statistical interpretation that other methods of faculty evaluation do not. Hodgkinson, who, as Dean of Bard College in New York State, created an evaluation model based on colleague evaluation, criticized:

> ...the privilege of locking the door of the college classroom while the instructor is lecturing. (It) is a tradition that interferes with proper assessment....If college and university teaching is to be professionalized, we must rely in large part on the professionals to develop better criteria for the assessment of this act. As far as I can tell, the only

conceivable way that college professors can do this is to get into the classroom, watch, and describe what goes on. The major virtues of this approach are that it encourages improved teaching and provides a means to establish criteria for assessment (p. 53).

A similar position was expressed by Eble (1972). Reporting his personal observations following visits, over a two-year period, to 70 colleges and universities, Eble asserted "there is no substitute for actual observation of a teacher in a classroom for judging how well he does this aspect of his job" (p. 60). Although he acknowledged the usefulness of classroom visitation, Eble also cited strenuous faculty resistance which, in his judgment, made highly unlikely the widespread adoption of classroom visitation as an evaluation procedure. He suggested that faculty resistance to classroom visitation was due to: (1) suspicions toward the visitor's intention, (2) uncertainty over the results, and (3) a sense of violation of professional standing.

Use of classroom visitation as an aspect of teaching evaluation has also been suggested by Miller (1972). In a position paper, he supported carefully planned classroom visitation as a technique that could provide needed appraisal data. Citing different classroom teaching styles, however, Miller cautioned that "care must be taken that the observer does not screen the teacher's performance too much through his own selective perceptions of what constitutes good teaching" (p. 31).

Opinion regarding the use of classroom visitation by faculty colleagues for the purpose of evaluating teaching performance, however, has not been uniformly favorable. Some educators have issued position papers that were sharply critical of the use of classroom visitation as an evaluative technique.

Gage (1961), for example, asserted that "...when the teacher knows he is being watched by someone whose opinion will determine his promotion or salary, his performance may depend more on his nerve than on his teaching skill" (p. 19). Moreover, Gage pointed to both lack of adequate time and shortage of staff as further lessening the practical value of classroom visitation.

This position parallels that of Gustad (1966). He offered several specific reasons to support his view that classroom visitation was an inappropriate means of obtaining evaluative data. These included: (1) the problem of obtaining a large enough unbiased observations sample, the need to separate visits designed to improve classroom instruction from those designed to gather data for retention, promotion and tenure decisions, and the expense involved in so time consuming a project.

Winthrop (1966) strongly opposed classroom visitation by colleagues and cited an additional aspect of colleague evaluation which, in his opinion, ensured the worst level of intellectual conformity:

> Majority group members often assert that final judgment on an instructor's teaching must rest with his colleagues. The colleagues may never have visited the unpopular instructor's classroom, although, of course, even if they had their opinions would be likely to be even biased... (p. 263)

The use of colleague visitation to the classroom as a device for the evaluation of teaching was not looked upon favorably by Hunter (1969). In a position paper he pointed to the increasingly impractical nature of visitation due to heavy administration and faculty workload. In addition, Hunter warned of dangers to morale from a required evaluation visit. He suggested that:

> In a college setting, it (colleague visitation) has perhaps dubious value from the beginning. Even assuming mutual trust and confidence between the two parties, unless the visitor is prepared to return several times, his impressions will hardly constitute a sound basis for judging a teacher's effectiveness over a semester (p. 90).

Classroom visitation by faculty colleagues has been suggested by some educators as an important source of information on quality of teaching performance. There have been offered, however, equally strong arguments against such evaluation.

Although a substantial number of educators have expressed their personal views, research studies investigating the reliability and validity of classroom visitation by faculty colleagues for purposes of evaluating teaching performance have yet to be carried out.

Student Evaluation

Examination of the literature shows that while a moderate number of educators appear to favor models of teacher evaluation based on either self or colleague evaluation, most educators appear to support models of teacher evaluation based largely on student ratings.

Morton (1961), for example, indicated his view in favor of student evaluation and suggested that, in addition to written comments, students end the term with an oral discussion on the strong and weak points of the instructor. Morton cautioned, however, that student appraisal must be part of a larger overall procedure designed to evaluate teaching performance.

Not surprisingly, the National Student Association issued a statement which strongly endorsed student participation in the evaluation of teaching performance. Written by Werdell (1967), it concluded that "...there are strong signs that student course and teacher evaluation when thoughtfully administered is the best existing way to improve the teaching-learning experience" (pp. 5-6).

Citing the need for more meaningful evaluation, Renner (1967) suggested the placing of more weight on evaluation by students in the overall teaching appraisal system. He expressed his position in this manner:

> Those who really know the instructor best are his students. Despite their limitations, they only have had an opportunity to participate fully in his teaching endeavors. They are the only ones who know whether he has been effective (p. 12).

Renner urged that a faculty-approved appraisal system for student evaluation be developed within each college and university.

Schwartz (1968) concurred and in a background paper for the annual meeting of the American Council on Education indicated his view that students were competent judges of lectures, discussions and papers. For that reason, he expressed strong support for inclusion of student appraisal in the evaluation of teaching performance.

Slobin and Nicholas (1969) supported student evaluation and suggested its adoption as "a means of letting the cooks know how the guests respond to the food" (p. 244). Among the values of student ratings of teachers cited by these authors were:

> (1) To help the university select and maintain good teachers by carefully examining the record prior to hiring and promotion, and (2) to provide incentives for basing promotion at least partly on teaching proficiency (p. 244).

Gaff and Wilson (1970) suggested that student evaluation would provide a reliable source for the evaluation of teaching. They believed that students should serve as important sources of information in evaluation systems developed in the future.

Support for student evaluation of teaching performance has also come from Centra (1971), a research psychologist at Educational Testing Service. Speaking before an audience of the American Association for Higher Education, Centra noted that, in his opinion, substantial agreement exists among administrative, faculty and student ratings of teachers. For that reason, Centra urged colleges and universities to adopt systematic student appraisal as an integral part of their procedures for the evaluation of teaching performance.

An enthusiastic supporter of student evaluation, Eble (1972) viewed students as singularly important observers of teaching performance. He suggested that students' insights into teaching effectiveness were simply unavailable elsewhere. Eble stated his view in this manner:

> On balance, student evaluation of teaching seems to contribute important data to the reward system that is not easily available from other sources and it calls attention to faculty performance in a way that is likely to produce favorable results (p. 70).

Cautioning that student appraisal of teaching should have as its primary purpose the improvement of teaching performance, Miller (1972) nevertheless suggested that in his opinion, the results of student evaluation should also "...enter into judgments about merit increases, promotion, tenure, and institutional severance. It would be wrong not to use every piece of valid evidence to reach the fairest possible decision about personal evaluation" (p. 30).

At least one large university has now mandated student evaluations in matters of faculty appointment or promotion. In an April, 1972, memorandum to all Queensboro Community College faculty, President Kurt Schmeller referred to the decision of the New York City Board of Higher Education and stated that effective September, 1972, "all personnel actions will require student evaluations as a matter of Board Policy."

While a substantial number of researchers in higher education have in recent years suggested the adoption of faculty evaluation techniques that include student ratings, student appraisal has also drawn substantial criticism.

Gage (1961), for example, was highly critical of student evaluation. He asserted that "teachers should not be penalized because of conditions over which they have no control such as level of the course, size of the class, and whether the course is elective or required" (p. 17). Gage suggested that teachers of courses that were either lower-level, larger sized, or were required, generally received lower student ratings. For that reason, Gage urged that student evaluation of teaching performance not be used for purposes of contract renewal or promotion in rank decisions.

Citing the lack of maturity in most college students, Bryant (1967) suggested that, in his judgment, a professor teaching a required freshman course, which is filled with students who have to take it, is at a disadvantage in competition with a professor teaching an advanced elective course, which is filled with students who want to take it. Asserting that students should not be permitted to wield evaluative power, Bryant stated that "a professor should not be forced to put his career at the mercy of undergraduates and should be given an equal chance with his colleagues" (p. 328).

Kerlinger (1971) sharply criticized student evaluation of professors. He argued that such evaluation of professors is "outside of instruction and, as such, alienates professors... (causes) instructor hostility, resentment and distrust...and undermines professional autonomy" (p. 353). Kerlinger urged that results of student evaluations should not be published or used for administrative decisions such as contract renewal, promotion and tenure.

Anthony and Lewis (1972) suggested that, in their judgment, many systems of student evaluation "do not measure 'teaching effectiveness' at all, but merely measure instructional effectiveness in the classroom which is but one component of the teaching process" (p. 13). They do not, according to the authors, measure class discussion, student presentation, office counseling, the use of various media, and the entire learning environment.

Although many educators have argued the merits of student evaluation, a far smaller number have actually conducted research studies investigating the reliability or validity of student appraisal of teaching performance.

Recent studies examining the reliability of student evaluation of faculty teaching performance have shown similar results. Bryan (1966), investigating test-retest reliability using a sample of 76 classes of students in 38 institutions within the State of Michigan, found a correlation of .80 between the ratings given faculty members by current students and those previously given to the same professor by alumni. Sherman (1969), in an unpublished study on the characteristics of one small college faculty found an intercorrelation of .90 among various student evaluation instruments used to appraise the same teacher. He recommended that student evaluation of teaching performance be included in systematized appraisal of faculty members for the purpose of contract renewal and promotion in rank.

26

Eric Clearinghouse of Higher Education Report 10, (1971), after reviewing recent literature related to student evaluation of teaching performance concluded that:

Typical measures of split-half reliability consistently show that the instruments employed in student ratings have a high reliability. They have been checked and rechecked in different studies (p. 12).

Recent studies have investigated the validity of student evaluation of faculty teaching. Unlike the reliability studies which have shown uniformly positive results, studies concerned with validity of student evaluation have yielded diverse results.

Several validity studies have examined the relationship between the rating received by a faculty member and the grade the student evaluator expected to receive.

Langon (1966), citing the experience of the University of Washington with more than 30,000 evaluations over a 43-year period, reported that student evaluation of teaching performance was not related in a statistical way to the grade level anticipated by student evaluation.

A study by Steward and Malpass (1966), using a sample of 1975 students taught by 67 instructors at the University of Florida, found that students expecting higher marks graded their instructors substantially higher than those expecting lower grades. On the basis of their findings, the authors recommended that student evaluation of teaching performance should not be an integral part of faculty evaluation procedures.

Different findings were reported by Rayder (1968), as a result of his research using a sample of 4285 students at Colorado State College. No statistical relationship was found between the student evaluation of teaching performance and the grade level anticipated by the student.

In his review of the research carried out by the colleges he visited on their students' evaluations of teaching performance, Eble (1972), too, concluded that student evaluation of teaching performance was not meaningfully affected by the grade they expected to receive. He recommended that students participate directly in the systematic evaluation of teaching performance. Eble suggested that this could best be achieved through inclusion of formal student appraisal in procedures for faculty contract renewal and promotion in rank.

Several validity studies have been concerned with additional factors which might affect the appraisal by students of faculty teaching performance.

27

Kirchner (1969) sampled all 227 students in 10 sections of the same course at the University of Kentucky and found statistically significant differences between the results when administration of the student evaluation was by the class instructor as opposed to a neutral individual. Higher ratings were achieved when the survey was administered by the instructor.

Rodin and Rodin (1972) used a random sample of 293 students taking the same multisection course and found a negative correlation between the amount learned from an instructor and the students' evaluation of that instructor's teaching performance. The authors recommended that student evaluation of teaching performance not be used for purposes of faculty contract renewal or promotion in rank.

In summary, although some studies have demonstrated that student evaluation of faculty teaching performance has a high degree of reliability, other research studies have failed to find a correspondingly high degree of validity.

Research on the Evaluation of Teaching Performance

While many teaching evaluation methods have been proposed, research has been somewhat limited. Only a small number of nationwide studies have been conducted to determine the evaluation methods that are actually being utilized in colleges and universities to evaluate teaching performance.

Two of the more prominent studies in recent years have been sponsored by the American Council on Education. Comparison of the nationwide results obtained in the 1961 study of Gustad with those obtained by Astin and Lee in 1966 reveals certain changes over time in sources of information being used to evaluate teaching performance in liberal arts colleges. Both studies sampled the opinions of academic deans. Respondents numbered 272 in the Gustad study and 484 in the Astin and Lee investigation. In both studies the liberal arts college sample included those in urban and rural areas, as well as schools varying in size and selectivity.

Use of self-evaluation remained rather constant and was ranked eleventh in importance in 1961 and tenth in 1966 out of fifteen sources of information.

Systematic student ratings appear to have sharply declined in use. Where student ratings ranked fifth in frequency of use out of fifteen sources of information employed in the evaluation of teaching in 1961, by 1966 the rank had fallen to twelfth out of fifteen information sources.

Even more substantial has been the decline in the use of classroom visitation as a means for obtaining information.

Ranking second in frequency of use in a group of fifteen possible sources of information used for evaluation of teaching in 1961, in 1966 classroom visitation fell to fifteenth out of the fifteen in frequency of use.

Sources whose frequency of use has apparently increased during the 1961 to 1966 period include utilization of committee evaluation of teaching and analysis of faculty grade distributions.

It appears that a nationwide research study into the policies and procedures used in evaluating teaching performance has not been undertaken since the 1966 study by Astin and Lee.

Importance of Specific Teaching Behaviors

Considerable attention has been focused in recent years on the importance of specific teaching behaviors both as predictors of teaching effectiveness and also as criteria by which teaching performance can be evaluated.

Musella Rusch (1968) suggested the following behaviors as criteria for appraising the teaching performance of members of the faculty: (1) positive attitude toward subject; (2) positive attitude toward students; (3) knowledge of subject and organization of subject matter; (4) effective use of discussion and questions.

From an extensive list of teacher traits, Eble (1969) selected the ones which, in his opinion, were most essential for effective teaching. Among the desirable teacher traits that he selected were the following: (1) being a dynamic and energetic person; (2) explaining clearly; (3) using interesting styles of presentation and (4) appearing to enjoy teaching.

A large-scale study that centered on identifying criteria for effective teaching was completed by Perry (1969) for the University of Toledo's Office of Institutional Research. Frequency of response from more than thirteen thousand students, faculty and alumni of the University of Toledo formed the basis upon which the most important behaviors in effective teaching were determined. These included: (1) being well prepared for class; (2) establishing interest in the subject matter being taught; (3) demonstrating comprehensive subject knowledge; (4) using good teaching methods; and (5) constructing tests which reach for student understanding not memorization.

Other academic researchers, however, have concluded that in their opinion, attempts to determine specific criteria against which teacher effectiveness could be measured have met with failure.

Mitzel (1960), for example, suggested that, in his view, it was not possible to specify teaching traits that were essential to effective teaching:

...more than a half-century of research effort has not yielded meaningful, measurable criteria around which the majority of the nation's educators can rally. No standards exist which are commonly agreed upon as THE criteria of teacher effectiveness (p. 148).

Biddle (1964) concurred and reported his belief that despite substantial research efforts there has been little or no success in the identification of teaching behaviors or skills that serve as good predictors of teaching effectiveness. A similar opinion was offered by Neeley (1968). In his judgment no agreement exists among educational authorities with regard to what constitutes either a good teacher or a criterion by which effective teachers can be identified.

Examination of the literature and research cited reveals that there is a lack of agreement among educators as to whether essential teaching behaviors can be identified.

A thorough review of the literature failed to uncover a single reference about the differentiation of teaching behaviors for the purposes of using them in the determination of contract renewal as distinct from promotion in rank.

SUMMARY

Research and literature on the evaluation of teaching effectiveness in higher education have been reviewed in this chapter.

In summary, recent studies have demonstrated that evaluation of teaching performance is of central importance in providing a reasonable base for administrative decisions on promotions, salaries, and tenure.

Little uniformity was noted, however, in the evaluation practices that are currently used. Moreover, researchers were sharply divided on the relative merits of appraisals based largely on self, faculty colleague, or student evaluation. Broad philosophical disagreements exist with regard to the sources of information that should be used in evaluating teaching performance.

III

THE SUBJECTS, THE MATERIALS, AND THE PROCEDURES

This chapter has four purposes: (1) to report how the sample of liberal arts colleges and academic deans was selected for this investigation; (2) to describe the materials which were utilized for the research, specifically the Evaluation of Teaching Performance Questionnaire; (3) to describe the general procedures which were used in the preparation and distribution of the questionnaire; and (4) to describe the statistical procedures that were used to analyze the collected data.

SUBJECTS

The purpose of this study was the determination of the policies and practices employed to evaluate the teaching performance of faculty members in four hundred and ninety-one private liberal arts colleges in the United States. The sampling consisted of all schools in the population of accredited liberal arts colleges that were neither part of a university nor part of a public system of education, and were so listed in the Education Directory (1971), published by the United States Department of Education, Washington, D.C.

The identification of the administrator serving as academic dean in each liberal arts college in the population employed in this study was also made by consulting the Education Directory (1971).

MATERIALS

Questionnaire. A two-part questionnaire was distributed to obtain data about the policies and practices of liberal arts colleges regarding evaluation of the teaching performance of faculty members for purposes of salary increment and promotion in rank personnel decisions.

Part One. Part One of the questionnaire was developed in 1966 by the American Council on Education, Washington, D.C. to determine techniques for the evaluation of undergraduate instruction. It has been adopted in the current research study

31

with the permission of Dr. Alexander W. Astin, Director of Research, American Council on Education.

The purposes of Part One of the research instrument, as designed by the American Council on Education, and as utilized in the current investigation, were: (a) to collect information about the relative importance placed on classroom teaching in the evaluation of overall performance of faculty members, and (b) to determine the types of information upon which the actual evaluation of teaching performance is based. An additional purpose of Part One of the current research study is to compare the data obtained in the current research study with that obtained in the study done for the American Council on Education seven years ago by Astin and Lee. (See Appendix)

Instructions given in Part One of the current research questionnaire were identical to those given respondents in the Astin study. These instructions requested that respondents place a check mark in the appropriate column indicating the factors that were principally considered in their liberal arts college in evaluating the overall performance of a faculty member. The code for the scale was: (1) major factor, (2) minor factor, (3) not a factor, and (4) not applicable. Respondents were then asked to place a check mark in the appropriate column indicating the frequency with which specific types of information were used in their college to evaluate the teaching performance of a faculty member. The code for the scale was: (1) always used, (2) usually used, (3) seldom used, and (4) never used.

Respondents were also asked several questions pertaining to the use of rating forms and were requested to indicate their answer by checking yes or no. Due to a printing error question number thirty-two, a rating form question, was listed in the questionnaire as being in Part Two but, in actuality, it was part of the questionnaire developed in 1966 by Astin and Lee and was adopted for use in the current research with permission of the American Council on Education.

Part Two. Part Two of the questionnaire was developed specifically for this research investigation.

The purposes of Part Two of the research instrument were: (a) to obtain data about the personal judgment of responding academic deans regarding selected components for the evaluation of the teaching performance of faculty members, (b) to determine the level of satisfaction of these academic deans with policies and practices currently used to evaluate classroom teaching performance and his perception of the level of satisfaction of most of his faculty, and (c) to determine the extent to which the level of importance assigned to specific teaching behaviors for the purpose of contract renewal differs from the level of importance assigned to specific teaching behaviors for the purpose of promotion in rank. (See Appendix)

In Part Two of the research instrument, instructions given for personal judgment questions requested respondents to place a check mark at the appropriate point along a four-point Likert-style continuum, ranging from "strongly agree" to "strongly disagree."

Respondents were asked, in addition, to indicate the importance that they personally attached to each of four components that could be used in evaluating teaching performance by rank ordering them from "one" to "four". The components were: student evaluation of teaching performance, faculty colleague evaluation of teaching performance, self-evaluation of teaching performance, and chairman evaluation of teaching performance.

Part Two of the questionnaire also included several questions which asked respondents to place a check mark next to the response that most closely indicated the level of satisfaction they felt, and, in addition, the level of satisfaction they believed their faculty felt with current evaluation policies and practices for both contract renewal and for promotion in rank. Response alternatives were (1) satisfied with all policies and practices, (2) satisfied with most policies and practices, (3) satisfied with few policies and practices, and (4) satisfied with none of the policies and practices.

To determine the importance of specific teaching behaviors for contract renewal and also for promotion in rank, respondents were instructed to rate the level of importance, on a four-point Likert-style continuum, that their college assigned to each teaching behavior. Number one was most important and number four was least important.

After Part Two of the research instrument had been developed in draft form, it was submitted to a panel of specialists for review. The members of this panel included:

Dr. Logan Wilson, President Emeritus, American Council on Education, Washington, D.C.

Dr. Alexander W. Astin, Director of Research, American Council on Education and major researcher in the 1966 study investigating techniques used to evaluate faculty members in higher education.

33

Dr. Martin J. Kaufman, Office of Research, Department of Health, Education and Welfare, Washington, D.C.

Dr. Edward Tomeski, Associate Professor of Computer Management, Fordham University, Bronx, New York

Dean James H. MacNeill, College of Business Administration, Fordham University, Bronx, New York

Mr. L. Long, Statistical Staff Manager, American Telephone & Telegraph, New York

In discussions with each specialist, comments were sought on the following aspects of the research instrument:
1. Clarity of the instructions to respondents.
2. Clarity of questions.
3. Sequencing and presentation of questions.
4. Adequacy of the questions for obtaining data appropriate to the purposes of the investigation.

The investigator met individually with all members of the panel of specialists. Most of the panel members were positive in their appraisal of the instrument. Specific suggestions were made by Dr. Tomeski and Dean MacNeill regarding reduction of the number of pages in the questionnaire and, with the approval of the dissertation seminar professors, this was done. In its final form, the research instrument was reduced from five to three pages. Dr. Wilson and Dr. Kaufman each recommended expansion of the sample size from a proposed random sample of liberal arts colleges to all schools in the population of liberal arts colleges that were neither part of a university nor part of a public system of education. With the approval of the dissertation seminar professors this recommendation was accepted.

Dr. Astin suggested that the instructions to respondents in several questions in Part Two of the research instrument be re-worded for clarity. He also recommended that, before it was distributed nationally, the final form of the questionnaire be reviewed for relevance by several academic administrators. Both recommendations were adopted by the researcher, with the approval of the dissertation seminar professors.

College data. In addition to the information sought on the questionnaire pertaining to the policies and practices used to evaluate the teaching performance of faculty members, respondents, although they remained anonymous, were asked to provide certain college data for statistical purposes. They were asked to check the appropriate numerical range for their college regarding the number of full-time faculty as well as their average freshman college board scores. Numerical ranges for full-time faculty were: (1) 50 or less, (2) 51 - 100, (3) 101 - 150, (4) 151 or more. Numerical ranges for average freshman college scores were: (1) 475 or less, (2) 476 - 550, (3) 551 - 625, (4) 626 or more.

Additional college data were added to returned questionnaires by the researcher. These data were based on information listed in the Education Directory (1971) and included the geographical location of each responding institution, using an east, west, south, midwest distribution, as well as whether the institution was "independent" or had a religious affiliation.

PROCEDURES

After permission was obtained from the American Council on Education to reproduce selected segments of their 1966 study and the dissertation outline of the investigator had been approved by the university, the questionnaire and accompanying cover letter were professionally type-set and printed.

Distribution and collection of questionnaire. At the end of January, 1973, the individual serving as academic dean at each liberal arts institution in the sample was mailed a packet. It contained a copy of the questionnaire with a cover letter, and a stamped, self-addressed envelope. The cover letter was individually signed, with a brief handwritten note of appreciation at the bottom. (See Appendix.)

Each liberal arts college receiving the questionnaire was assigned a code number which was written on the outside of the return envelope.

At the end of February, 1973, a second copy of the questionnaire, original cover letter, and stamped, self-addressed envelope were mailed to those academic deans who had not yet responded, approximately four weeks after the initial mailing. Again, the cover letters were individually signed, with a brief handwritten note requesting an early response. (See Appendix.)

The return envelope carried the code number which had been assigned to each liberal arts college. The closing date for the acceptance of completed questionnaires was set as the second week of April, 1973.

The returned questionnaires were sent out for processing at the end of April, 1973. An IBM 360-40 data processing system was utilized.

Statistical analysis - Part One. The data obtained from the Evaluation of Teaching Performance Questionnaire were analyzed by different methods according to the part under consideration.

35

Data from Part One of the research instrument were analyzed in the following manner:

1. Frequency of response was determined for each sub-category in the following classifications: (a) four numerical ranges relating to the size of the full-time faculty of responding institutions, (b) four numerical ranges relating to the average freshman college board scores of responding institutions, (c) four geographic regions relating to the location of responding institutions, and (d) two sub-categories relating to whether or not each responding institution was religiously affiliated.

2. To determine the evaluation factors that are considered in evaluating the overall performance of members of the faculty, frequency and percentage of response for each evaluation factor were computed and analyzed for all responding institutions combined.

3. To determine the degree to which different types of information were used to evaluate the teaching performance of faculty members, frequency and percentage of response for each of the different types of information were computed and analyzed for all responding liberal arts colleges.

4. To determine whether there were statistically significant differences between results regarding evaluation factors obtained in the 1966 Astin and Lee study and those obtained in the current investigation, "t" tests were utilized (Dixon and Massey, 1957, pp. 232 - 233). Although the data obtained in the Astin and Lee study for column 2, "minor factor," column 3, "not a factor," and column 4, "not applicable," were not available, data from the Astin and Lee study for column 1, "major factor," were available and were compared with data obtained in the current research study under the "major factor" category.

5. To determine whether there were significant differences in the types of information used to evaluate teaching performance between the frequency of response for column 1, "always used," obtained in 1966 by Astin and Lee and comparable data in the current investigation, "t" tests were employed.

6. Frequency and percentage of response were obtained and analyzed in order to determine whether special rating forms were used in collecting data on teaching competence. Frequency and percentage of response were also obtained to determine the amount of research being conducted concerning the validity or usefulness of these rating forms.

Statistical analysis - Part Two. Data obtained from Part Two of the research instrument were analyzed in the following manner:

1. To determine the personal judgment of academic deans

regarding questions relating to the evaluation of teaching performance, frequency and percentage of response on a four-point Likert-type scale were obtained for all responding academic deans.

2. To determine the relative importance that academic deans, themselves, placed on components that could be used in the evaluation of a faculty member's teaching performance, the frequency and percentage of their responses at each of four ranks were computed.

3. To determine the differences in satisfaction with policies for evaluation between deans and faculty, frequency and percentage of response were computed for four levels of satisfaction. Frequency and percentage of response were computed for deans and faculty at four levels of satisfaction separately for contract renewal and promotion in rank.

4. To determine the number of liberal arts colleges applying a checklist of written criteria for evaluation of teaching performance for contract renewal or promotion in rank, frequency and percentage of response were obtained.

5. To determine the level of importance assigned by all liberal arts colleges to specific teaching behaviors for purposes of contract renewal and for promotion in rank, frequency and percentage of response on a four-point Likert-type scale were obtained.

6. To determine whether there were differences between the importance assigned by liberal arts colleges to different teaching behaviors in evaluating faculty teaching performance for purposes of contract renewal as opposed to promotion in rank, frequency and percentage of response to category "most important" were determined for both contract renewal and promotion in rank.

7. To determine the degree to which the responses by academic deans indicate the assignment of identical levels of importance to individual teaching behaviors when used for purposes of either contract renewal or promotion in rank, percentages were obtained.

All data obtained in this research investigation were subjected to an IBM 360 - 40 data system.

IV

THE FINDINGS

The purpose of this chapter is to analyze and to report the responses of academic deans on a two-part questionnaire dealing with the policies and procedures used in the evaluation of teaching performance in liberal arts colleges. Part One of the questionnaire was a replication of selected segments of the Astin and Lee (1966) study for the American Council on Education. Part Two of the questionnaire was developed to provide additional information regarding the evaluation of teaching performance.

The first section of this chapter presents the total response returns of the questionnaire sent to the academic deans of liberal arts colleges. The liberal arts colleges comprising the sample were not part of a university or part of a state-supported system of higher education.

Data and analyses from Part One of the questionnaire are presented in the second section of this chapter. These data and analyses include the following: (1) percentage of response of academic deans to levels of importance of criteria used in evaluating overall faculty performance, (2) percentage of response of academic deans to frequency of use of types of information considered in evaluating teaching performance.

Certain selected aspects of the Astin and Lee (1966) study were available and are compared in this section with similar data from the current research study: (1) percentage of response to criteria identified by academic deans as "major factors" in evaluating overall faculty performance, (2) t-tests of differences in percentage of response to criteria identified as "major factors" in evaluating overall faculty performance, (3) percentage of response to types of information identified by academic deans as "always used" in evaluating faculty teaching performance, (4) t-tests of differences in percentage of response to types of information identified by academic deans as "always used" in evaluating faculty teaching performance, (5) percentage of response of colleges reporting use of and research on validity of rating forms used to evaluate faculty teaching performance.

The final section of this chapter reports data and analyses from Part Two of the questionnaire. These data and analyses from Part Two include the following: (1) percentage of response of academic deans to an opinion questionnaire pertaining to the evaluation of faculty teaching performance, (2) rank ordering by academic deans of four components used in the evaluation of faculty teaching performance, (3) percentage of response of academic deans indicating their level of satisfaction and the estimated level of satisfaction of their faculty with policies and practices for contract renewal and promotion in rank, (4) number of liberal arts colleges applying a checklist of written criteria for evaluation of teaching performance for contract renewal or promotion in rank, (5) percentage of response to levels of importance of teaching behaviors for the purpose of contract renewal and promotion in rank, (6) percentage of response to category "most important" in teaching behaviors used for purposes of contract renewal and promotion in rank, (7) percentage of academic deans whose reports indicate the assignment of identical levels of importance to individual teaching behaviors used for purposes of contract renewal and promotion in rank.

PERCENTAGE OF RESPONSE TO QUESTIONNAIRE

Table 1 reports the total number of questionnaires distributed, the total returned and the percentage of returns.

A total of 83.5 percent (410 of 491) of the questionnaires was returned by academic deans of liberal arts colleges. Some variation occurred in the rate of response within each classification of liberal arts colleges. With regard to "size of faculty," nearly 90.0 percent (192 of 215) of the institutions with a faculty size of 51 - 100 responded, while there was response from 56.0 percent (14 of 25) of institutions with 151 or more faculty. Liberal arts colleges with "average freshman college board scores" of 475 or less had a response rate of 72.4 percent (113 of 156), while 94.9 percent (56 of 59) of those institutions with average college board scores of 551 - 625 responded.

The rate of response for liberal arts colleges having a "religious affiliation" was 81.3 percent (256 of 315) as opposed to 87.5 percent (154 of 176) for liberal arts colleges not having a religious affiliation. Rate of response was approximately 87.0 percent for colleges in the south (113 of 130) or midwest (149 of 169) and approximately 76.0 percent for colleges in the east (114 of 147) or west (34 of 45).

The analyses of the data that follow are, therefore, based upon 83.5 percent of the total group, with differing percentages of respondents represented in the sub-categories.

TABLE 1

PERCENTAGES OF RETURNS OF QUESTIONNAIRES SENT TO ACADEMIC DEANS OF LIBERAL ARTS COLLEGES

Classification of Liberal Arts College	Total Sent	Total Returns	Percentage of Returns
Size of Faculty			
1. 50 or less	189	155	82.0
2. 51 - 100	215	192	89.3
3. 101 - 150	62	49	79.0
4. 151 or more	25	14	56.0
Average Freshman College Board Scores			
1. 475 or less	156	113	72.4
2. 476 - 550	258	225	87.2
3. 551 - 625	59	56	94.9
4. 626 or more	18	16	88.9
Religious Affiliation or Not			
1. Yes	315	256	81.3
2. No	176	154	87.5
Geographical Location			
1. East	147	114	77.6
2. West	45	34	75.6
3. South	130	113	86.9
4. Midwest	169	149	88.2
Total	491	410	83.5

TABLE 2

PERCENTAGES OF RESPONSE BY ACADEMIC DEANS TO LEVELS OF IMPORTANCE OF
CRITERIA USED IN EVALUATION OF FACULTY PERFORMANCE FOR PROMOTION
IN RANK, SALARY INCREASE OR TENURE DECISION IN
LIBERAL ARTS COLLEGES
(N=410)

Criteria	(1) Major Factor	(2) Minor Factor	(3) Not A Factor	(4) Not Applicable
1. Classroom teaching	99.3	0.7	0.0	0.0
2. Supervision of graduate study	1.9	6.5	4.2	87.3
3. Supervision of honors program	2.9	24.9	19.0	53.2
4. Research	22.2	60.7	12.4	4.6
5. Publication	17.1	69.5	10.7	2.7
6. Public service	12.9	70.5	13.7	2.9
7. Consultation	0.7	43.9	41.5	13.0
8. Activity in professional societies	15.8	74.4	8.8	0.9
9. Student advising	68.8	28.1	2.7	0.5
10. Campus committee work	49.5	48.1	1.2	0.9
11. Length of service in rank	54.4	40.2	3.7	1.7
12. Competing job offers	3.2	31.5	56.3	9.0
13. Personal attributes	53.2	40.5	4.9	1.5

ANALYSIS OF QUESTIONNAIRE: PART ONE

Data and analyses from Part One of the questionnaire include the following: (1) percentage of response of academic deans to levels of importance of criteria used in evaluating overall faculty performance, (2) percentage of response of academic deans to frequency of use of types of information considered in evaluating teaching performance.

Certain select aspects of the Astin and Lee (1966) study were available and were compared with the following results of the current research study: (1) percentage response of criteria identified by academic deans as "major factors" in evaluating overall faculty performance, (2) t-tests of difference in percentage of response to criteria identified as "major factors" in evaluating overall faculty performance, (3) percentage of response to types of information identified by academic deans as "always used" in evaluating faculty teaching performance, (4) t-tests of difference in percentage of response to types of information identified by academic deans as "always used" in evaluating faculty teaching performance, (5) percentage of response of colleges reporting use of and research on validity of rating forms used to evaluate faculty teaching performance.

Analysis of data from current study: Table 2 presents the percentage of response by academic deans of liberal arts colleges to levels of importance of criteria used to evaluate faculty performance.

Classroom teaching was listed as a "major factor" in evaluating overall faculty performance by 99.3 percent of responding academic deans. Other items which were rated as being a "major factor" by approximately 50 percent or more of the respondents included the following: "student advising", 68.8 percent; "length of service in rank, 54.4 percent; "personal attributes", 53.2 percent and "committee work", 49.5 percent.

Rated as a "minor factor" by 50 percent or more of responding academic deans were: (1) "professional societies," (2) "public service," and (3) "publication." Each was rated a "minor factor" by approximately 70 percent of respondents. In addition, "research" was rated as a "minor factor" by 60.7 percent of responding deans.

"Consultation" and "competing job offers" were rated as "not a factor" in evaluating overall faculty performance by 41.5 percent and 56.3 percent of respondents respectively. "Supervision of graduate study" and "supervision of honors program" were rated as "not applicable" to evaluating overall faculty performance by 87.3 percent and 53.2 percent of respondents, respectively.

TABLE 3

PERCENTAGES OF RESPONSE OF ACADEMIC DEANS TO FREQUENCY OF USE OF
TYPES OF INFORMATION CONSIDERED IN EVALUATING
TEACHING PERFORMANCE
(N=410)

Types of Information	(1) Always Used	(2) Usually Used	(3) Seldom Used	(4) Never Used
1. Systematic student ratings	29.3	30.2	30.0	10.5
2. Informal student opinions	17.8	61.2	19.5	1.5
3. Classroom visits	5.1	15.6	55.9	23.4
4. Colleagues' opinions	39.8	45.9	13.4	0.9
5. Scholarly research and publication	19.5	40.5	30.9	9.0
6. Student examination performance	3.7	20.2	53.4	22.7
7. Chairman evaluation	85.4	10.5	0.9	3.2
8. Dean evaluation	85.4	10.9	2.9	0.7
9. Course syllabi and examinations	10.5	33.2	45.9	10.5
10. Long term follow-up of students	2.2	13.7	53.2	30.9
11. Enrollment in elective courses	2.9	34.9	42.9	19.3
12. Alumni opinions	1.9	10.7	63.7	23.7
13. Committee evaluations	42.2	18.3	19.8	19.8
14. Grade distributions·	2.4	18.5	50.5	28.5
15. Self-evaluation or report	20.0	25.4	32.2	22.4

A small number of respondents specified "other" factors in question 14 that were used in their liberal arts college in evaluating the overall performance of a faculty member for promotion in rank, salary increase, or tenure. These responses did not lend themselves to computer analysis, since the number was so small. Consequently, the investigator read each response to question 14 and categorized the varied replies. Among additional factors cited in the evaluation of overall faculty performance were the following:

(1) academic preparation
(2) scholarship
(3) advanced degrees
(4) cooperative spirit
(5) devotion to duty
(6) service to college
(7) creativity
(8) self-improvement
(9) productivity

In summary, while a large percentage of the colleges reported that teaching and student advising were "major" factors in evaluating faculty performance, there was less uniformity in the response to other criteria as "major" factors. Similarly, while a large percentage of colleges reported that research, publication, public service and professional societies were "minor" factors in faculty evaluation, there was less agreement on the assignment of other criteria to the "minor" category.

Table 3 presents the percentage of response of academic deans of liberal arts colleges to frequency of use of types of information considered in evaluating faculty teaching performance.

Types of information, which were rated as being "always used" by 50 percent or more of responding liberal arts colleges included the following: (1) "chairman evaluation", 85.4 percent; and (2) "dean evaluation", 85.4 percent.

Rated as "always" or "usually" used in evaluation of teaching performance by 50 percent or more of responding liberal arts colleges were the following types of information: (1) "colleagues' opinions," 85.7 percent; (2) "informal student opinions," 79.0 percent; (3) "committee evaluation," 60.5 percent; (4) "scholarly research and publication," 60.0 percent, and (5) "systematic student ratings," 59.5 percent.

The following types of information were rated as being either "seldom" or "never" used by 50 percent or more of responding liberal arts colleges: (1) "alumni opinions," 87.4 percent; (2) "long term follow-up of students," 84.1 percent; (3) "classroom visits," 79.3 percent; (4) "grade distributions,"

44

TABLE 4

t-TESTS OF DIFFERENCES IN PERCENTAGES OF RESPONSE TO CRITERIA
IDENTIFIED BY ACADEMIC DEANS AS "MAJOR FACTORS" IN
EVALUATING OVERALL FACULTY PERFORMANCE AS
REPORTED IN THE ASTIN AND LEE (1966)
STUDY AND THE CURRENT STUDY (1973)

Factors	1966 (N=484) Percentage	1973 (N=410) Percentage	t
1. Classroom teaching	97.6	99.3	2.36
2. Supervision of graduate study	17.8	1.9	8.57
3. Supervision of honors program	14.3	2.9	6.46
4. Research	31.7	22.2	3.24
5. Publication	24.5	17.1	2.75
6. Public service	16.1	12.9	1.37
7. Consultation (government, business)	2.4	0.7	2.36
8. Activity in professional societies	23.9	15.8	3.08
9. Student advising	46.8	68.8	6.85
10. Campus committee work	32.6	49.5	5.21
11. Length of service in rank	59.9	54.4	1.66
12. Competing job offers	9.8	3.2	4.19
13. Personal attributes	61.3	53.2	2.59

$t_{.05}=1.96$

$t_{.01}=2.57$

79.0 percent; (5) "student examination performance," 76.1 percent; (6) "enrollment in elective courses," 62.2 percent; (7) "course syllabi and examinations," 56.4 percent; (8) "self-evaluation or report," 54.6 percent.

Use of "systematic student ratings" appears to be quite diverse. While approximately 60 percent of responding institutions indicated that they "always" or "usually" used systematic student ratings, approximately 40 percent indicated that they "seldom" or "never" use "systematic student ratings" in evaluating the teaching performance of members of the faculty. "Informal student opinions," however, are "always" or "usually" used by approximately 80 percent of liberal arts colleges while approximately 20 percent reported that they "seldom" or "never" use "informal student opinions."

Use of "self-evaluation or report" in evaluating teaching performance appears to vary considerably among liberal arts colleges. Approximately 45 percent of responding institutions indicated that they "always" or "usually" use "self-evaluation or report" while approximately 55 percent indicated that they "seldom" or "never" use that type of information in evaluating teaching effectiveness.

A very small number of respondents specified "other" types of information that were used in their liberal arts college in evaluating the teaching performance of faculty members. The small number of responses did not permit computer analysis. Consequently, the investigator read all such responses and categorized the varied replies. Additional types of information cited included the following:

(1) scholarship
(2) innovation
(3) productivity
(4) advanced degrees

In summary, the data from the research study as presented in Table 3, indicates that large percentages of liberal arts colleges depend upon Chairman Evaluation and Dean Evaluation of faculty performance most of the time.

Comparison of data from the current study and the Astin and Lee study. Where the findings of the Astin and Lee (1966) study were available, they were compared with the results obtained in the current research study.

Table 4 reports the percentage response of criteria identified in 1966 and in 1973 by academic deans of liberal arts colleges as "major factors" in evaluating overall faculty performance.

"Classroom Teaching" was rated as a major factor in evaluating overall faculty performance by nearly every responding academic dean in both the 1966 and 1973 surveys. Comparable percentages are 97.6 and 99.3 percent, respectively. Two other factors received a rating of 50 percent or more in both surveys. They were "length of service in rank," which was rated as a major factor by 59.9 percent of the academic deans in 1966 and 54.4 percent of the academic deans in 1973; and "personal attributes," which was rated as a major factor by 61.3 percent of the academic deans in 1966 and 53.2 percent of the academic deans in 1973.

Differences of more than ten percent between the 1966 and 1973 ratings were observed in four factors. Declining in ratings by more than ten percent were "supervision of graduate study" and "supervision of honors programs" which declined from 1966 ratings of 17.8 percent and 14.3 percent respectively to 1.9 percent and 2.9 percent respectively in the 1973 study. Increasing in ratings by more than ten percent were "student advising" and "campus committee work" which increased from 1966 ratings of 46.8 percent and 32.6 percent, respectively, to 68.8 percent and 49.5 percent, respectively in the 1973 study.

Smaller percentage changes between the 1966 and 1973 surveys were recorded for the following factors: (1) "research" declined from a 1966 rating of 31.7 percent to a 1973 rating of 22.2 percent, (2) "publication" declined from 24.5 percent in 1966 to 17.1 percent in the 1973 study, (3) "activity in professional societies" declined from a 1966 rating of 23.9 percent to a 1973 rating of 15.8 percent, and (4) "public service" declined from 16.1 percent in 1966 to 12.9 in the 1973 study.

Two other factors, "consultation" and "competing job offers" declined slightly in percentage rating and, in addition, were rated as a "major factor" in evaluating overall faculty performance by less than four percent of academic deans.

It is quite apparent that the findings of the 1973 study regarding criteria used to evaluate overall faculty performance varied considerably from the findings of the Astin and Lee (1966) study. In order to examine further the extent of the differences in the percentages of response to criteria identified by academic deans of liberal arts colleges as "major factors," t-tests of the differences between mean percentages were computed.

While t-tests may be more appropriate to smaller samples than those in the current study, Mr. L. Long, Statistical Staff Manager, American Telephone and Telegraph Company, and statistical consultant to the current research project, recommended that, according to Dixon and Massey (1957), pp. 232-3, the t-test was an appropriate statistic for analysis of these data and those reported in Table 7. In their text, Introduction to

TABLE 5
t-TESTS OF DIFFERENCES IN PERCENTAGES OF RESPONSE TO TYPES OF
INFORMATION IDENTIFIED BY ACADEMIC DEANS IN THE ASTIN
AND LEE (1966) STUDY AND THE CURRENT STUDY (1973)
AS "ALWAYS USED" IN EVALUATING FACULTY
TEACHING PERFORMANCE

Types of Information	1966 (N=484) Percentage	1973 (N=410) Percentage	t
1. Systematic student ratings	11.2	29.3	6.84
2. Informal student opinions	47.2	17.8	10.14
3. Classroom visits	9.8	5.1	2.76
4. Colleagues' opinions	50.6	39.8	3.28
5. Scholarly research and publication	36.6	19.5	5.86
6. Student examination performance	24.7	3.7	9.81
7. Chairman evaluation	82.2	85.4	1.30
8. Dean evaluation	83.5	85.4	.78
9. Course syllabi and examinations	29.4	10.5	7.47
10. Long term follow-up of students	9.9	2.2	5.08
11. Enrollment in elective courses	14.0	2.9	6.39
12. Alumni opinions	11.2	1.9	5.91
13. Committee-evaluation	28.9	42.2	4.18
14. Grade distributions	36.0	2.4	14.73
15. Self-evaluation or report	15.4	20.0	1.80

$t_{.05} = 1.96$

$t_{.01} = 2.57$

48

Statistical Analysis, Dixon and Massey, in referring to the difference in proportions, cited an example which compared the opinions of 400 people in one city to the opinions of 500 people in a different city. Those sample sizes are comparable to the ones utilized in the current research study.

The results of the t-tests are also reported in Table 4.

Analysis of the data indicated significant differences at the .01 level between the mean percentages of each of nine faculty evaluation factors in 1966 and in 1973. The nine factors were as follows: (1) "supervision of graduate study," (2) "supervision of honors program," (3) 'research," (4) "publication," (5) "activity in professional societies," (6) "student advising," (7) "campus committee work," (8) "competing job offers," and (9) "personal attributes."

Significant differences at the .05 level were found between the mean percentages of each of two faculty evaluation factors in 1966 and in 1973. The two factors were as follows: (1) "classroom teaching," and (2) "consultation (government, business)."

Analysis of the percentage ratings given in 1966 and in 1973 to two faculty evaluation factors, "public service" and "length of service in rank," indicated no significant differences.

Thus, in eleven of the thirteen instances, it may be stated that the mean percentages obtained in the two studies are from different distributions.

Table 5 presents the percentage of response to types of information identified by academic deans as "always used" in evaluating faculty teaching performance as reported in the Astin and Lee (1966) study and the current study.

Changes of 20 percent or more in the responses to the 1966 and 1973 surveys found in the category "always used" were: (1) "informal student opinions" decreased from 47.2 percent in 1966 to 17.8 percent in the 1973 survey, (2) "student examination performance" decreased from 24.7 percent in the earlier study to 3.7 percent in the 1973 survey, (3) "grade distributions" decreased from 36.0 percent in the 1966 survey to 2.4 percent in the current survey.

Changes of 15 percent but less than 20 percent in the responses to the 1966 and 1973 surveys were recorded for the following types of information that were cited as "always used" in evaluating the teaching performance of faculty members: (1) "systematic student ratings" increased from 11.2 percent in 1966 to 29.3 percent in the 1973 survey, (2) "scholarly research and publication" decreased from a 1966 rating of 36.6 percent to a 19.5 percent, (3) "course syllabi and examination" decreased from 29.4 percent in the earlier study to 10.5 percent in the present study, and (4) "committee evaluation" increased from 28.9 percent in the 1966 study to 42.2 percent in the 1973 study.

In comparing results of the 1966 and 1973 studies, changes of 10 percent or more but less than 15 percent were recorded for the following types of information that were cited as "always used" in evaluating the teaching performance of faculty members: (1) "enrollment in elective courses" declined from 14.0 percent in the earlier study to 2.9 percent in the current study, and (2) "alumni opinions" declined from 11.2 percent in the earlier survey to 1.9 percent in the 1973 survey.

Changes of less than 10 percent in the responses to the 1966 and 1973 surveys were recorded for the following types of information that were cited as "always used" in evaluating the teaching performance of faculty members: (1) "classroom visits" declined from 9.8 percent in the 1966 survey to 5.1 percent in the 1973 survey, (2) "long term follow-up of students" declined from 9.9 percent in the earlier survey to 2.9 percent in the present survey, (3) "self-evaluation or report" increased from a 1966 rating of 15.4 percent to a 1973 rating of 20.0 percent.

Table 5 has reported data which suggests that substantial changes have occurred since the 1966 Astin and Lee survey of the types of information identified by academic deans as "always used" in evaluating faculty teaching performance.

To determine the statistical significance of these changes, $\underline{t}$-tests were computed for the differences in mean percentages of response to types of information identified by academic deans of liberal arts colleges in the Astin and Lee (1966) study and the current study as "always used" in evaluating faculty teaching performance. They are also presented in Table 5.

Analysis of these data indicated significant differences at the .01 level between the mean percentage obtained for each of twelve types of information used to evaluate the teaching performance of faculty members in the 1966 and 1973 studies. The twelve types of information were as follows: (1) "systematic student ratings," (2) "informal student opinions," (3) "classroom visits," (4) "colleagues' opinions," (5) "scholarly research and publication," (6) "student examination performance," (7) "course syllabi and examinations," (8) "long term follow-up of students," (9) "enrollment in elective courses," (10) "alumni opinions," (11) "committee evaluation," and (12) "grade distributions."

Analysis of the data indicated no significant differences between the mean percentages obtained in the 1966 survey and those obtained in the 1973 survey for each of the following types of information used in evaluating teaching performance:

(1) "chairman evaluation," (2) "dean evaluation," and (3) "self-evaluation or report."

In summary, significance tests of the differences between ratings of twelve of the fifteen types of information indicate that, in these instances, the mean percentages obtained in the 1966 and 1973 surveys are from different distributions.

Table 6 presents the percentages of liberal arts colleges reporting frequency of use of rating forms to evaluate faculty teaching performance and research on the validity of these rating forms in the Astin and Lee (1966) study and in the current 1973 study.

TABLE 6

PERCENTAGES OF ACADEMIC DEANS REPORTING FREQUENCY OF USE OF RATING FORMS TO EVALUATE FACULTY TEACHING PERFORMANCE AND RESEARCH ON THE VALIDITY OF RATING FORMS IN THE ASTIN AND LEE (1966) STUDY AND IN THE CURRENT (1973) STUDY

	1966 (N=484)	1973 (N=410)
Frequency of use of rating forms	23.9	54.9
Research performed on rating forms	0.6	8.3

A substantial increase appears to have occurred in the use of rating forms to evaluate the teaching performance of faculty members in liberal arts colleges. While fewer than one school in four reported use of rating forms in the 1966 survey by Astin and Lee, more than one half of the schools surveyed in 1973 reported use of rating forms in evaluating teaching performance.

The percentage of liberal arts colleges reporting that they have done research on the validity of their rating forms has also increased. In the 1966 Astin and Lee survey, 0.6 percent reported the existence of research on their rating forms, as contrasted with 8.3 percent in the current 1973 survey.

In summary, many more liberal arts colleges indicated in the 1973 study that they are using rating forms than indicated so in the 1966 study. In addition, there is an increase in the number of colleges reporting research validation of their rating forms since the 1966 study by Astin and Lee.

ANALYSIS OF QUESTIONNAIRE: PART TWO

In Part Two of the questionnaire no comparison of data with results found in the Astin and Lee (1966) study was possible, since questions in Part Two were developed as part of this research study. The following data will be analyzed in Part Two: (1) percentage of response of academic deans to an opinion questionnaire pertaining to the evaluation of faculty teaching performance, (2) rank ordering by academic deans of four components used in the evaluation of faculty teaching performance, (3) percentage of response of academic deans indicating their level of satisfaction and estimated satisfaction level of their faculty with policies and practices for contract renewal and promotion in rank, (4) number of liberal arts colleges applying a checklist of written criteria for evaluation of teaching performance for contract renewal or promotion in rank, (5) percentage of response to levels of importance of teaching behaviors for the purpose of contract renewal and promotion in rank, (6) percentage of response to category "most important" in teaching behaviors used for purposes of contract renewal and promotion in rank, (7) percentage of academic deans whose responses indicate the assignment of identical levels of importance to individual teaching behaviors used for purposes of contract renewal and promotion in rank.

Table 7 reports the percentage of responses by academic deans of liberal arts colleges to questions relating to their opinions about the evaluation of faculty teaching performance.

Nearly 70 percent of the academic deans indicated disagreement with the statement suggesting that "the results of systematic student evaluation of a faculty member's teaching performance indicate more about a teacher's popularity than about his teaching performance".

Disagreement was expressed by nearly 74 percent of the academic deans to the statement suggesting that the "results of systematic student evaluation of a faculty member's teaching performance should be made public." Approximately 46 percent of the academic deans indicated "strong disagreement" with the statement.

Nearly 80 percent of the academic deans indicated disagreement with the statement suggesting that "systematic and planned classroom visitation by faculty colleagues for the purpose of evaluating a faculty member's teaching performance is an invasion of academic privacy."

52

In the opinion of approximately 85 percent of the academic deans, "results of an institutionalized, uniform approach to faculty self-evaluation should be one of the most important components in evaluation of faculty teaching performance." Approximately 50 percent of the 85 percent of the academic deans responding positively indicated "strong agreement" with the statement.

Approximately 70 percent of the academic deans indicated agreement with the statement suggesting that "the academic personnel policies and practices used to evaluate a faculty member's teaching position are well known by most members of the faculty." "Strong agreement" with this statement was indicated by 28 percent of responding academic deans.

Disagreement was expressed by approximately 60 percent of the academic deans with the statement "academic personnel decisions made in liberal arts colleges are based primarily on objective information (that is, information that is rational, impersonal and unprejudiced)."

In summary, almost half of the academic deans responding held strong opinions about three of the six statements. About half of the respondents strongly agreed that "results of an institutionalized, uniform approach to faculty self-evaluation should be one of the important components in evaluation of faculty teaching performance," and strongly disagreed that "the results of systematic student evaluation of a faculty member's teaching performance should be made public," and "systematic and planned classroom visitation by faculty colleagues for the purpose of evaluating a faculty member's teaching performance is an invasion of academic privacy."

Table 8 reports the personal opinions of academic deans regarding the rank order of importance of four components used in the evaluation of faculty teaching performance.

"Chairman evaluation" was ranked first in importance in the opinion of 44.2 percent of the academic deans of liberal arts colleges. "Student evaluation" was ranked first in importance by 23.7 percent of the responding deans. "Faculty evaluation" was ranked first in importance by 21.5 percent of the academic deans. "Self-evaluation" was ranked first in importance in the opinion of 10.7 percent of responding academic deans of liberal arts colleges.

The component most frequently ranked first in importance was "chairman evaluation," which was ranked first by 44.2 percent of the academic deans. The component most frequently ranked second in importance was "faculty colleague evaluation" which was ranked second by 34.6 percent of the academic deans.

TABLE 7

PERCENTAGES OF RESPONSE BY ACADEMIC DEANS OF LIBERAL ARTS COLLEGES
TO OPINION QUESTIONS ABOUT THE EVALUATION OF
FACULTY TEACHING PERFORMANCE
(N=410)

QUESTIONNAIRE ITEMS	PERCENTAGES			
	Strongly Agree 1	2	3	Strongly Disagree 4
1. The results of systematic student evaluation of a faculty member's teaching performance indicate more about a teacher's popularity than about his teaching performance.	5.4	26.6	49.8	18.3
2. The results of systematic student evaluation of a faculty member's teaching performance should be made public.	7.8	18.3	27.8	46.1
3. Systematic and planned classroom visitation by faculty colleagues for the purpose of evaluating a faculty member's teaching performance is an invasion of academic privacy.	7.1	14.4	32.7	45.9
4. Results of an institution-alized, uniform approach to faculty self-evaluation should be one of the important components in evaluation of faculty teaching performance.	50.5	34.6	12.4	2.4
5. The academic personnel policies and practices used to evaluate a faculty member's teaching performance are well known by most members of the faculty.	28.1	41.2	23.2	7.6
6. Academic personnel decisions made in liberal arts colleges are based primarily on objective information (that is, information that is rational, impersonal and unprejudiced).	3.9	35.9	42.2	18.1

The component most frequently ranked third in importance by responding academic deans was "student evaluation" which was ranked third by 30.5 percent of respondents. The component most frequently ranked fourth in importance in the opinion of academic deans of liberal arts colleges was "self-evaluation," which was ranked fourth by 53.9 percent of responding academic deans.

TABLE 8

PERCENTAGES OF ACADEMIC DEANS RANKING IMPORTANCE OF
FOUR CRITERIA USED IN THE EVALUATION OF
FACULTY TEACHING PERFORMANCE

| Criteria | PERCENTAGES | | | |
| | RANK ASSIGNED TO CRITERIA | | | |
	First	Second	Third	Fourth
Student Evaluation	23.7	29.3	30.5	16.6
Faculty Colleague Evaluation	21.5	34.6	26.6	17.3
Self-Evaluation	10.7	11.5	23.9	53.9
Chairman Evaluation	44.2	24.6	19.0	12.2

In summary, almost half of the responding academic deans assigned greatest importance to the chairman's evaluation. More than half the deans assigned least importance to self-evaluation.

Table 9 reports the percentage of academic deans of liberal arts colleges indicating their level of satisfaction and the estimated level of satisfaction of their faculty with the policies and practices used in their college for faculty contract renewal and promotion in rank.

The opinion of the academic deans as well as their estimate of the view of most of their faculty indicate that, in the perception of academic deans, there is substantial satisfaction with the policies and practices used to evaluate faculty for both contract renewal and also for promotion in rank. Nearly 80 percent of academic deans indicated satisfaction with "all" or "most" of the policies and practices regarding contract renewal. A slightly lower figure, approximately 75 percent of the deans, indicated that they were satisfied with "all" or "most" of the evaluation policies and practices regarding promotion in rank.

The academic deans estimated that nearly 93 percent of their faculty were satisfied with "all" or "most" of the policies and practices used to evaluate teaching performance for purposes of contract renewal. A slightly lower estimate of faculty satisfaction was recorded with regard to promotion in rank, with approximately 86 percent of the deans estimating that most of their faculty were satisfied with "all" or "most" of the evaluation policies and practices.

The academic deans personal level of satisfaction with policies and practices was somewhat lower than their estimate of that of most of their faculty. With regard to contract renewal, 79 percent of the deans indicated satisfaction with "all" or "most" of the policies and practices. They estimated that approximately 92 percent of their faculty were satisfied with "all" or "most" of the contract renewal policies and practices. For promotion in rank, approximately 75 percent of the deans indicated satisfaction with "all" or "most" of the policies and practices. They estimated that nearly 87 percent of their faculty were satisfied with "all" or "most" of the promotion in rank policies and practices. Nearly 21 percent of the academic deans indicated that they were satisfied with "few" or "none" of the evaluation of teaching performance policies and practices for purposes of contract renewal. This contrasts with the deans' estimate that approximately 7 percent of their faculty were satisfied with "few" or "none" of the contract renewal policies and practices. Approximately 25 percent of the academic deans indicated that they were satisfied with "few" or "none" of the evaluation of teaching performance policies and practices for purposes of promotion in rank. This contrasts with the estimate of the deans that approximately 13 percent of their faculty were satisfied with "few" or "none" of the promotion in rank policies and practices.

The level of satisfaction most frequently selected by academic deans personally and in their estimation of the opinions of their faculty was, "satisfied with most policies and practices." This was true for purposes of both contract renewal and promotion in rank.

In summary, the data reported in Table 9 indicates a high level of satisfaction, on the part of academic deans, with policies and practices relating to promotion in rank. The academic deans

TABLE 9

PERCENTAGES OF RESPONSE OF ACADEMIC DEANS TO LEVELS OF SATISFACTION
WITH THE POLICIES AND PRACTICES USED IN THEIR COLLEGE FOR
CONTRACT RENEWAL AND PROMOTION IN RANK
(N=410)

	Percentages			
	Dean's Personal Level of Satisfaction		Dean's Estimate of Level of Satisfaction of Faculty	
Level of Satisfaction	Contract Renewal	Promotion In Rank	Contract Renewal	Promotion In Rank
Satisfied with all policies and practices.	10.7	9.3	6.8	4.9
Satisfied with most policies and practices.	68.3	65.9	85.6	81.7
Satisfied with few policies and practices.	20.2	24.6	7.1	13.2
Satisfied with none of policies and practices.	0.7	0.7	0.5	0.2

indicated that, in their estimation, members of their faculty were even more satisfied than the deans, themselves, with policies and practices for contract renewal and promotion in rank.

Table 10 reports the number of liberal arts colleges applying a checklist of written criteria in evaluating teaching performance for purposes of contract renewal and for promotion in rank.

Use of written criteria in the evaluation of teaching performance for purposes of contract renewal was reported by approximately 25 percent of responding liberal arts colleges.

A somewhat larger percentage of institutions, nearly 37 percent, indicated that they use a checklist of written criteria when evaluating teaching performance for purposes of promotion in rank.

TABLE 10

NUMBER AND PERCENTAGES OF LIBERAL ARTS COLLEGES APPLYING A
CHECKLIST OF WRITTEN CRITERIA FOR THE EVALUATION
OF TEACHING PERFORMANCE
(N=410)

Evaluation For:	Number	Percentage of total response
Contract Renewal		
Colleges using written criteria	104	25.4
Colleges not using written criteria	306	74.6
Promotion in Rank		
Colleges using written criteria	151	36.8
Colleges not using written criteria	259	63.2

Table 11 reports the percentage of response of academic deans of liberal arts colleges to levels of importance of teaching behaviors used for purposes of contract renewal and promotion in rank.

A high degree of similarity was evident between the level of importance assigned to teaching behaviors used in the evaluation of teaching performance for purposes of contract renewal

58

and for purposes of promotion in rank. Few of the behaviors were rated by large percentages of respondents at the "least important" end of the continuum.

The following behaviors were rated on the "most important" half of the continuum (intervals 1 and 2), in the evaluation of teaching performance by 90 percent or more of the responding academic deans, whether the evaluation was for contract renewal or for promotion in rank: (1) "is well prepared for class," (2) "demonstrates comprehensive subject knowledge," (3) "motivates students to do their best," (4) "encourages intelligent independent thought by students," (5) "treats students with respect," (6) "discusses points of view other than his own," (7) "communicates effectively to the level of his students," and (8) "is fair and reasonable to students in grading procedures."

Rated on the "most important" half of the continuum by 70 percent to 90 percent of the academic deans were the following teaching behaviors: (1) "is dynamic and energetic person," and (2) "seems to enjoy teaching."

For purposes of contract renewal, the teaching behavior rated at the "most important" end of the continuum by the largest number of academic deans was "communicates effectively to the level of his students," which was rated by 98.3 percent of deans "most important." The teaching behavior for purposes of contract renewal that was rated at the "least important" end of the continuum by the largest number of academic deans was "is dynamic and energetic person," rated "least important" by 25.8 percent of the deans.

With regard to promotion in rank, the teaching behavior rated at the "most important" end of the continuum by the largest number of deans was "demonstrates comprehensive subject knowledge," which was rated as "most important" by 97.6 percent of responding deans. The teaching behavior that was rated at the "least important" end of the continuum for purposes of promotion in rank by the largest number of academic deans was "is dynamic and energetic person," rated "least important" by 21.9 percent of the deans.

In summary, the data reported in Table 11 indicate that the level of importance attached to teaching behaviors for purposes of contract renewal is very similar to the level of importance attached to the same teaching behaviors for purposes of promotion in rank. In addition, most of the academic deans responding assigned a high level of importance to all of the teaching behaviors listed.

In order to facilitate closer examination of the assignment to the "most important" end of the continuum of the teaching

TABLE 11

PERCENTAGES OF RESPONSE OF ACADEMIC DEANS TO LEVELS OF
IMPORTANCE OF TEACHING BEHAVIORS USED FOR PURPOSES
OF CONTRACT RENEWAL AND PROMOTION IN RANK

| | PERCENTAGES | | | |
| | Contract Renewal | | | |
Teaching Behaviors	Most Important 1	2	3	Least Important 4
Is well prepared for class	69.8	28.3	1.79	0.2
Demonstrates comprehensive subject knowledge	67.8	30.0	2.24	0.0
Motivates students to do their best	69.0	27.3	3.49	0.2
Encourages intelligent independent thought by students	59.3	31.5	7.84	1.5
Treats students with respect	59.8	34.9	5.14	0.2
Discusses points of view other than his own	41.5	44.9	12.4	1.2
Is dynamic and energetic person	26.6	27.6	23.4	2.4
Seems to enjoy teaching	40.0	41.9	16.6	1.5
Communicates effectively to the level of his students	68.3	30.0	1.5	0.2
Is fair and reasonable to students in grading procedures	57.1	37.6	4.6	0.7

TABLE 11 (continued)

Teaching Behaviors	PERCENTAGES Promotion In Rank			
	Most Important 1	2	3	Least Important 4
Is well prepared for class	68.5	29.0	2.2	0.3
Demonstrates comprehensive subject knowledge	73.9	23.7	2.4	0.4
Motivates students to do their best	68.5	26.1	5.1	0.2
Encourages intelligent independent thought by students	60.5	31.7	6.8	0.9
Treats students with respect	59.5	34.6	5.4	0.5
Discusses points of view other than his own	43.9	43.7	10.5	1.9
Is dynamic and energetic person	30.7	47.3	19.5	2.4
Seems to enjoy teaching	43.2	41.5	14.2	1.2
Communicates effectively to the level of his students	65.9	30.7	3.2	0.2
Is fair and reasonable to students in grading procedures	56.8	36.8	5.4	0.9

61

behaviors listed by the responding academic deans, the data in this category from Table 11 are presented side by side in Table 12.

Little difference was noted between the level of importance assigned by liberal arts colleges to teaching behaviors evaluated for purposes of contract renewal as contrasted with the level of importance assigned to teaching behaviors evaluated for purposes of promotion in rank.

The level of importance assigned to teaching behaviors appears to depend more on the specific teaching behavior in question rather than whether that teaching behavior is to be used in the evaluation of teaching for purposes of contract renewal or promotion in rank.

Summarizing the data in Table 11 and 12, three separate groupings of levels of importance assigned to teaching behaviors may be defined, for both purposes of contract renewal and promotion in rank. The teaching behaviors and the groupings are:

Highest importance (more than 65 percent): "Is well prepared for class," "motivates students to do their best," "communicates effectively to the level of his students," and "demonstrates comprehensive subject knowledge."

Medial importance (from 50 percent to 65 percent): "Treats students with respect," "encourages intelligent independent thought by students," and "is fair and reasonable to students in grading procedure."

Lowest importance (under 50 percent): "Discusses points of view other than his own," "seems to enjoy teaching," and "is dynamic and energetic person."

For nine of the ten teaching behaviors, the percentage of deans of liberal arts colleges who rated a particular teaching behavior at the "most important" end of the continuum for purposes of contract renewal was within four percentage points of the rating given the same teaching behavior for purposes of promotion in rank. The nine teaching behaviors and the percentage of deans who rated each teaching behavior as "most important" for contract renewal and for promotion in rank are as follows: (1) "is well prepared for class," 69.8 and 68.5 percent; (2) "motivates students to do their best," 69.0 and 68.5 percent; (3) "communicates effectively to the level of his students," 68.3 and 65.9 percent; (4) "treats students with respect," 59.8 and 59.5 percent; (5) "encourages intelligent independent thought by students," 59.3 and 60.5 percent; (6) "is fair and reasonable to students in grading procedure," 57.1 and 56.8 percent; (7)

TABLE 12

PERCENTAGES OF RESPONSE TO TEACHING BEHAVIORS IDENTIFIED BY
ACADEMIC DEANS AS "MOST IMPORTANT" IN EVALUATING
TEACHING PERFORMANCE FOR CONTRACT
RENEWAL AND PROMOTION IN RANK
(N=410)

Teaching Behaviors	Contract Renewal	Promotion in Rank
Is well prepared for class	69.8	68.5
Demonstrates comprehensive subject knowledge	67.8	73.9
Motivates students to do their best	69.0	68.5
Encourages intelligent independent thought by students	59.3	60.5
Treats students with respect	59.8	59.5
Discusses points of view other than his own	41.5	43.9
Is dynamic and energetic person	26.6	30.6
Seems to enjoy teaching	40.0	43.2
Communicates effectively to the level of his students	68.3	65.9
Is fair and reasonable to students in grading procedure	57.1	56.8

"discusses points of view other than his own," 41.5 and 43.9 percent; (8) "seems to enjoy teaching," 40.0 and 43.2 percent; (9) "is dynamic and energetic person," 26.6 and 30.6 percent.

The other teaching behavior, "demonstrates comprehensive subject knowledge" was rated as "most important" by 67.8 percent of the liberal arts colleges when used for purposes of contract renewal and by 73.9 percent when used for purposes of promotion in rank. The difference between the ratings for this teaching behavior was approximately six percentage points.

In order to obtain a more precise measure of the extent of the similarity between the levels of importance assigned behaviors used to evaluate teaching performance for purposes of contract renewal and for purposes of promotion in rank, the percentage of responding academic deans indicating identical levels of importance for behaviors when used for purposes of contract renewal and for promotion in rank were calculated. They are presented in Table 13.

Table 13 reports the percentage of academic deans whose responses indicate that their college assigns identical levels of importance to teaching behaviors used to evaluate teaching performance for purposes of contract renewal and promotion in rank.

The level of importance assigned by the academic deans, to each of the teaching behaviors, was quite similar whether such behaviors were being used in the evaluation of teaching for the purpose of contract renewal or for the purpose of promotion in rank.

Approximately 91 percent of the academic deans reported that their liberal arts college assigned the same level of importance to the teaching behavior, "is well prepared for class," when used in the evaluation of teaching either for purposes of contract renewal or for purposes of promotion in rank. Similar percentages were recorded for the following teaching behaviors: (1) "is fair and reasonable to students in grading procedures," 90.4 percent; (2) "communicates effectively to the level of his students," 89 percent; and (3) "treats students with respect," 88.8 percent.

Slightly lower percentages were accorded the following teaching behaviors: (1) "motivates students to do their best," 86.8 percent; (2) "demonstrates comprehensive. subject knowledge," 85.1 percent; (3) "seems to enjoy teaching," 85 percent; (4) "encourages intelligent independent thought by students," 82.2 percent; and (5) "is dynamic and energetic person," 81.0 percent.

Table 11 and Table 12 presented data relating to the importance of specific teaching behaviors in the evaluation of teaching

TABLE 13

PERCENTAGE OF ACADEMIC DEANS ASSIGNING IDENTICAL LEVELS OF IMPORTANCE
TO BEHAVIORS USED TO EVALUATE TEACHING PERFORMANCE FOR PURPOSES
OF CONTRACT RENEWAL AND PROMOTION IN RANK
(N=410)

Teaching Behaviors	Percentage
Is well prepared for class	91.2
Demonstrates comprehensive subject knowledge	85.1
Motivates students to do their best	86.8
Encourages intelligent independent thought by students	82.2
Treats students with respect	88.8
Discusses points of view other than his own	84.1
Is dynamic and energetic person	81.0
Seems to enjoy teaching	85.0
Communicates effectively to the level of his students	89.0
Is fair and reasonable to students in grading procedures	90.4

performance for purposes of both contract renewal and promotion in rank.   Few differences were noted in the level of importance assigned teaching behaviors when used for contract renewal and the level of importance assigned when used for promotion in rank.   There were, however, differences in the levels of importance assigned by the academic deans to the individual teaching behaviors, for both contract renewal and promotion in rank.   Three separate groupings of importance of teaching behaviors were defined.   Table 13 provided further information that indicates a high percentage of responding academic deans view the teaching behaviors necessary for contract renewal to be the same as the teaching behaviors necessary for promotion in rank.

It should be noted that while differences were of both practical and statistical significance in many cases, there are limitations upon the findings as a function of the rate of response. For example, in Table 2, while 99.3 percent responded classroom teaching was a "major factor," this reflects 99.3 percent of the 83.5 percent of academic deans who responded. The opinions of the 16.5 percent who did not respond are not included. Therefore, the rate of return must be taken into consideration as one examines the data.

V

SUMMARY, CONCLUSIONS, AND RECOMMENDATIONS

This chapter includes the following: (1) a summary of the investigation, (2) the method of procedure, (3) findings of the research study, and (4) conclusions and suggestions for further research.

SUMMARY

Purpose of the study. The major purpose of this study was to determine the current policies and practices used in liberal arts colleges to evaluate classroom teaching performance of members of the faculty for the purposes of providing information to be used in making decisions regarding retention, salary increment, and promotion in rank. The secondary purpose was to compare current policies and practices with those described in 1966 by Astin and Lee in their study of policies and practices used to evaluate classroom teaching performance.

Specifically, this study proposed to answer the following questions:

1. To what extent is quality of teaching performance considered a major factor in the evaluation of overall faculty performance in liberal arts colleges?

2. From what specific sources do academic deans of liberal arts colleges obtain data to evaluate the teaching performance of individual members of the faculty?

3. To what extent are rating forms or other instruments employed to gather information on the quality of teaching performance of individual members of the faculty in liberal arts colleges?

4. What are the personal judgments of academic deans about methods of evaluating faculty teaching performance that rely primarily on students, faculty colleagues, department chairmen or faculty self-evaluation as sources of information for the evaluation of a faculty member's teaching performance?

5. To what degree do the academic deans of liberal arts

colleges express satisfaction with the policies and practices used in their colleges to evaluate the classroom teaching performance of faculty members?

6. To what degree are written criteria used to measure and evaluate the teaching performance of faculty members in decisions of promotion in rank and contract renewal?

7. Which behavioral criteria of teaching are rated most important in evaluating faculty teaching performance in decisions of promotion in rank and contract renewal?

8. To what extent do the policies and practices used to evaluate faculty teaching performance for purpose of contract renewal differ from the policies and practices used to evaluate faculty teaching performance for purpose of promotion in rank?

9. To what extent have changes occurred in the policies and practices used in liberal arts colleges to evaluate the classroom teaching performance of faculty members since the survey by Astin and Lee (1966)?

Subjects and materials. The sample used for this study consisted of all schools in the population of accredited liberal arts colleges that were neither part of a university nor part of a public system of education. Status was determined on the basis of the category placement of the institution in the Education Directory (1971), published by the United States Department of Education, Washington, D.C.

The administrator serving as academic dean in each liberal arts college in the population employed in this study was also identified from lists published in the Education Directory (1971).

The data gathering instrument consisted of a two-part questionnaire. Part One of the questionnaire was developed in 1966 by the American Council on Education, Washington, D.C. to determine techniques for the evaluation of undergraduate instruction. It was adopted in the current research study in consultation with Dr. Alexander W. Astin, Director of Research, American Council on Education.

The purposes of Part One of the research instrument, as designed by the American Council on Education, and as utilized in the current investigation, were: (a) to collect information about the relative importance placed on classroom teaching in the evaluation of overall performance of faculty members, and (b) to determine the types of information upon which the actual evaluation of teaching performance is based. An additional purpose of Part One of the questionnaire was to compare the data obtained in the current research study with that obtained in the study done for the American Council on Education seven years ago by Astin and Lee. (See Appendix.)

Instructions given in Part One of the current research questionnaire were identical to those given participants in the Astin and Lee study.

Part Two of the questionnaire was developed specifically for this research investigation.

The purposes of Part Two of the research instrument were: (a) to obtain data about the personal judgment of responding academic deans regarding selected components for the evaluation of teaching performance of faculty members, (b) to determine the level of satisfaction of these academic deans with policies and practices currently used to evaluate classroom teaching performance, (c) to determine the academic dean's perception of the level of satisfaction of most of his faculty, and (d) to determine the extent to which the level of importance assigned to specific teaching behaviors for the purpose of contract renewal differs from the level of importance assigned to specific teaching behaviors for the purpose of promotion in rank.

Procedures. After Part Two of the research instrument had been developed in draft form, it was submitted to a panel of specialists in higher education for review. Recommended modifications were incorporated.

At the end of January, 1973, the individual serving as academic dean at each liberal arts institution in the sample was mailed a packet. It contained a copy of the questionnaire with a cover letter and a stamped, self-addressed envelope. The cover letter was individually signed with a brief handwritten note of appreciation at the bottom. (See Appendix.)

Each liberal arts college receiving the questionnaire was assigned a code number. This number was handwritten on the outside of the return envelope.

At the end of February, 1973, approximately four weeks after the initial mailing, a second copy of the questionnaire and the original cover letter, and a stamped, self-addressed envelope was mailed to those academic deans who had not yet responded. Again, the cover letters were individually signed, with a brief handwritten note requesting an early response. (See Appendix.)

The return envelope for the second mailing carried the code number which had been assigned to each liberal arts college. The closing date for the acceptance of completed questionnaires was set as the second week of April, 1973.

Data analysis. The returned questionnaires were processed at the end of April, 1973. An IBM 360 - 40 data processing system was utilized.

The data obtained from Part One of the questionnaire was

analyzed in the following manner: (1) to determine the extent to which quality of teaching performance is considered a major factor in the evaluation of overall faculty performance, percentages of response to levels of importance of criteria used to evaluate faculty performance were computed and analyzed; (2) to determine specific types of information from which academic deans of liberal arts colleges obtain data to evaluate the teaching performance of individual members of the faculty, percentages of response to frequency of use of types of information considered in evaluating faculty teaching performance were computed and analyzed; (3) to determine the level of significance of the differences between the percentages of response to criteria identified by academic deans as "major factors" in evaluating overall faculty performance in the current study and the earlier Astin and Lee (1966) study, t-tests (Dixon and Massey, 1957) were computed; (4) to determine the level of significance of the differences between the percentages of response to types of information identified by academic deans as "always used" in evaluating faculty teaching performance in the current study and the earlier Astin and Lee (1966) study, t-tests (Dixon and Massey, 1957) were computed; (5) to determine the extent to which rating forms were used to evaluate faculty teaching performance and the extent of research on those rating forms, frequencies and percentages were computed for the current study and were compared with frequencies and percentages reported in the Astin and Lee (1966) study.

The data obtained from Part Two of the questionnaire were analyzed in the following manner: (1) to determine the personal judgments of academic deans about methods that employ students, faculty colleagues, department chairmen or faculty self-evaluation as sources of information for the evaluation of a faculty member's teaching performance, percentages of response to questionnaire items covering these methods were computed and analyzed; (2) to determine the relative importance, in the opinion of responding academic deans, of four components frequently used to evaluate the teaching performance of faculty members, average rank order of the components was computed and analyzed; (3) to determine the level of satisfaction which academic deans express with policies and practices for contract renewal and promotion in rank and their perceptions of the level of satisfaction of their faculty with these policies and practices, percentages of response at four levels were computed and analyzed; (4) to determine the degree to which written criteria were used to measure and evaluate the teaching performance of faculty members in decisions of promotion in rank and contract renewal, frequencies of response at two levels were computed and analyzed; (5) to determine the levels of importance given teaching behaviors for the purposes of contract renewal and for promotion in rank, percentages at four levels were computed and analyzed; (6) to determine the extent to which the policies and practices used to evaluate faculty teaching performance for purposes of contract renewal differed from the policies and practices used to evaluate faculty teaching performance for purposes of promotion in rank, percentages of response to category "most important" in teaching behaviors were computed and analyzed; (7) to determine the degree to which academic deans assigned identical levels of importance to teaching behaviors for purposes of contract renewal and promotion in rank, percentages of response to four levels were computed and analyzed.

The minimum level of statistical significance accepted in the study was .05.

Findings, Part One. Part One of the questionnaire replicated selected segments of the Astin and Lee (1966) study of the techniques used to evaluate the teaching performance of faculty members on the undergraduate level of instruction.

1. An analysis of the levels of importance of criteria used in the overall evaluation of faculty performance indicated the following:

    a. "Classroom teaching" was listed as a "major factor" by 99.3 percent of responding academic deans.

    b. Other criteria rated as "major factors by approximately 50 percent or more of the academic deans included (1) "student advising," (2) "length of service in rank," (3) "personal attributes," and (4) "committee work."

    c. Rated as "minor factors" by 50 percent or more of the academic deans were (1) "professional societies," (2) "public service," (3) "publication," and (4) "research."

2. An analysis of the types of information considered in evaluating the teaching performance of faculty members indicated the following:

    a. Rated as "always used" by 50 percent or more of the academic deans were: (1) "chairman evaluation," and (2) "dean evaluation."

    b. Rated as "always" or "usually" used in evaluating teaching performance by 50 percent or more of the academic deans included: (1) "colleagues' opinions," (2) "informal student opinion, ; (3) "committee evaluation," (4) "scholarly research and publication," and (5) "systematic student ratings."

    c. Rated as "seldom" or "never" used by 50 percent or more of the academic deans were: (1) "alumni opinions,"

(2)"long term follow-up of students," (3)"classroom visits," (4)"grade distributions (5)"student examination performance," (6)"enrollment in elective course," (7)"course syllabi and examinations," and (8)"self-evaluation or report."

d. Approximately 60 percent of the academic deans indicated that their institutions "always" or "usually" use "systematic student ratings," while approximately 40 percent indicated that they "seldom" or "never" use "systematic student ratings."

e. "Informal student opinions" are "always" or "usually" used by approximately 80 percent of the liberal arts colleges, according to their academic deans, while approximately 21 percent reported that they "seldom" or "never" use "informal student opinions."

3. A comparison of the responses by academic deans to criteria identified in the Astin and Lee (1966) study and included in the present study as "major factors" in evaluating overall faculty performance indicated the following:

a. There were statistically significant differences (t.01-2.57) between mean percentages of response obtained in the 1966 Astin and Lee study and the current study on nine of thirteen criteria used to evaluate the overall performance of faculty members. The direction of the differences between mean percentages of response for the Astin and Lee study and the current study, that reached levels of significance, are as follows: (1) "supervision of graduate study" decreased, (2) "supervision of honors programs" decreased, (3) "research" decreased, (4) "publications" decreased, (5) "activity in professional societies" decreased, (6) "student advising" increased, (7) "campus committee work" increased, (8) "competing job offers" decreased, and (9) "personal attributes" decreased.

b. There were statistically significant differences (t.05-1.96) between mean percentages of response obtained in the 1966 Astin and Lee study and the current study on two of the thirteen criteria used to evaluate the overall performance of faculty members. The direction of the differences between mean percentages for the Astin and Lee study and the current study that reached levels of significance are as follows: (1) "classroom teaching" increased, and (2) "consultation" decreased.

c. "Classroom teaching" was rated as a "major factor" by nearly every academic dean in both the 1966 study (97.6 percent) and the current research study (99.3 percent).

d. Other criteria which received a rating as a "major

factor" by 50 percent or more deans in both studies were "length of service in rank" and "personal attributes."

e. A decline of more than 10 percent between the 1966 and 1973 ratings was recorded for "supervision of graduate study" and "supervision of honors programs."

f. An increase in ratings of more than 10 percent between the 1966 and 1973 ratings was recorded for "student advising" and "campus committee work."

g. A decline of less than 10 percent between the 1966 and 1973 ratings was recorded by "research," "publication," "activity in professional societies," and "public service."

4. An analysis of the response to types of information identified by academic deans as "always used" in evaluating faculty teaching performance as reported in the Astin and Lee (1966) study and the current study indicated the following:

a. There were statistically significant differences at the .01 level for eleven of fourteen types of information used to evaluate the teaching performance of faculty members when a t-test comparison was made between the data obtained in the 1966 Astin and Lee study and the current 1973 study. The direction of the differences between mean percentages of response for the Astin and Lee study and the current study that reached levels of significance are as follows: (1) "systematic student ratings" increased, (2) "informal student opinions" decreased, (3) "classroom visits" decreased, (4) "colleagues' opinions" decreased, (5) "scholarly research and publication" decreased, (6) "student examination performance" decreased, (7) "course syllabi and examinations" decreased, (8) "long term follow-up of students" decreased, (9) "alumni opinions" decreased, (10) "committee evaluations" increased, and (11) "grade distributions" decreased.

b. Decreases of 20 percent or more were found for three types of information including "informal student opinions," "student examination performance," and "grade distributions."

c. Decreases of more than 15 but less than 20 percent were found for two types of information used to evaluate faculty teaching performance. They were: (1) "scholarly research and publication" and "course syllabi and examinations." Increases of more than 15 but less than 20 percent were found for two types of information used to evaluate faculty teaching performance. They were: (1) "systematic student ratings" and (2) "committee evaluation."

d. Decreases of less than 15 percent were found for four types of information including: (1) "enrollment in elective courses," (2) "alumni opinions," (3) "classroom visits," and

(4) "long term follow-up of students." An increase of less than 15 percent was found for "self-evaluation or report."

5. An analysis of the percentage of academic deans who reported in the Astin and Lee (1966) study and in the current study that their liberal arts college used rating forms to evaluate faculty teaching performance indicated the following:

a. While fewer than one school in four reported use of rating forms in the 1966 study by Astin and Lee (23.9 percent), more than half of the schools in 1973 (54.9 percent) reported use of rating forms in evaluating teaching performance.

b. The percentage of academic deans reporting that their liberal arts college has done research on the validity or usefulness of their rating forms has increased from 0.6 percent in the 1966 study by Astin and Lee to 8.3 percent in the current study.

Findings, Part Two. Part Two of the questionnaire was developed for this research study to provide additional information related to the policies and practices used to evaluate the teaching performance of members of the faculty.

1. An analysis of the response of academic deans to personal judgment questions pertaining to the evaluation of faculty teaching performance indicated the following:

a. Academic deans indicated strong agreement (50.5 percent) with the statement suggesting that results of an institution-alized, uniform approach to faculty self-evaluation should be an important component in evaluation of teaching per-formance.

b. Strong disagreement was indicated by 46.1 percent of the academic deans to the statement suggesting that results of systematic student evaluation of faculty teaching performance should be made public.

c. Strong disagreement was indicated by 45.9 percent of the academic deans to the statement suggesting that planned classroom visitation by faculty colleagues for the purpose of evaluating teaching performance was an invasion of academic privacy.

2. An analysis of the rank ordering by academic deans of four components used in the evaluation of faculty teaching perfor-mance indicated the following:

a. Approximately 45 percent of the academic deans assigned greatest importance to the "chairman evaluation."

b. "Student evaluation," "faculty evaluation," and "self-evaluation" were assigned lower importance than "chairman evaluation" with 23.7 percent, 21.5 percent and 10.7 percent, respectively.

c. The most frequent rank ordering was "chairman evaluation," "student evaluation," "faculty evaluation," and "self-evaluation."

3. An analysis of the response of academic deans reporting their level of satisfaction and the estimated level of satisfaction of their faculty with policies and practices for contract renewal and promotion in rank indicated the following:

a. Substantial satisfaction (approximately 77 percent) with the policies and practices used to evaluate faculty for purposes of contract renewal and for promotion in rank was reported by academic deans. Their estimate of the view of most of their faculty was that approximately 89 percent were satisfied with "all" or "most" policies and practices for contract renewal and promotion in rank.

b. The academic deans' opinion regarding level of satisfaction as indicated above, was somewhat lower than their estimate of the opinion of most of their faculty.

c. The academic deans indicated a slightly higher level of satisfaction regarding policies and practices of faculty evaluation for purposes of contract renewal (79 percent) than for promotion in rank (75.2 percent).

d. The estimate by the academic deans of the level of satisfaction of most of their faculty indicated that, in the perception of the academic deans, their faculty was slightly more satisfied with policies and practices of faculty evaluation for purposes of contract renewal (92.4 percent) than for promotion in rank (86.6 percent).

4. An analysis of the number of academic deans who indicated that their liberal arts college applied a checklist of written criteria for evaluation of teaching performance for contract renewal or promotion in rank indicated the following:

a. Use of a checklist of written criteria in their liberal arts college for the evaluation of teaching performance for purposes of contract renewal was reported by approximately one of every four academic deans (25.4 percent).

b. Slightly more than one of every three academic deans (36.8 percent) reported use of a checklist of written criteria for purposes of promotion in rank in their liberal arts college.

5. Analysis of the response to levels of importance of teaching behaviors for the purpose of contract renewal and promotion in rank indicated the following:

a. A high degree of similarity was evident between the levels of importance assigned to teaching behaviors used in the evaluation of teaching performance for purposes of contract renewal and for purposes of promotion in rank. For example, the teaching behavior "is well prepared for class" was rated on the "most important" half of the continuum (intervals 1 and 2) by 98.1 percent of the academic deans when used for purposes of contract renewal and by 97.5 percent of the deans when used for purposes of promotion in rank. Similarly, the teaching behavior "treats students with respect" was rated on the "most important" half of the continuum by 94.7 percent of the academic deans when used for contract renewal and by 94.1 percent of the deans when used for purposes of promotion in rank.

b. Eight of the ten teaching behaviors were rated at the "most important" side of the continuum by 90 percent or more of the academic deans whether such teaching behaviors were for evaluation of contract renewal or for promotion in rank.

c. For purposes of contract renewal the teaching behavior rated "most important" by the largest number of academic deans (98.3 percent) was "communicated effectively to the level of his students."

d. With regard to promotion in rank, the teaching behavior rated "most important" by the largest number of academic deans (97.6 percent) was "demonstrates comprehensive subject knowledge."

6. Further analysis of the above data, examining only teaching behaviors rated on the continuum at the "most important" end of the continuum in evaluation for purposes of contract renewal as contrasted with promotion in rank, indicated the following:

a. For nine of the ten teaching behaviors, the percentage of academic deans reporting that their liberal arts college rated a particular teaching behavior category at the "most important" end of the continuum for purposes of contract renewal was within four percentage points of the rating given the same teaching behavior for purposes of promotion in rank.

b. For purposes of both contract renewal and promotion in rank, the three teaching behaviors rated on the continuum at the "most important" end by the largest number of academic deans were "is well prepared for class" (69.8 percent for contract renewal, 68.5 percent for promotion in rank), "motivates students to do their best" (69.0 percent for contract renewal and 68.5 percent for promotion in rank), and "communicates effectively to the level of his students" (68.3 percent for contract renewal and 65.9 percent for promotion in rank).

7. An analysis of the reports of academic deans whose response suggested that their college assigned identical levels of importance to distinct teaching behaviors used to evaluate teaching performance for purposes of contract renewal and promotion in rank indicated that for all ten teaching behaviors, more than 80 percent of the academic deans reported that their liberal arts college assigned each teaching behavior the identical level of importance in evaluating teaching performance for contract renewal and for promotion in rank.

CONCLUSIONS

On the basis of the findings of this research investigation concerning the current policies and practices used in liberal arts colleges to evaluate the classroom teaching performance of members of the faculty for the purposes of making academic personnel decisions such as retention, salary increment and promotion in rank, the following conclusions seem warranted:

1. The vast majority of liberal arts colleges place major importance on quality of teaching performance in the evaluation of an individual faculty member's overall performance.

2. In addition to "classroom teaching," the criteria of "student advising," "length of service in rank," "personal attributes," and "committee work" are used by the majority of liberal arts colleges in the evaluation of overall faculty performance.

3. The primary sources from which information is obtained for use in evaluating faculty teaching performance are "chairman evaluation" and "dean evaluation." Other sources of information used in a majority of colleges include: (a) "colleagues' opinions," (b) "informal student opinions," (c) "committee evaluation," (d) "scholarly research and publication," and (e) "systematic student ratings."

4. Considerable difference of opinion exists among academic deans in their ranking, in order of importance, of four components used in the evaluation of faculty teaching performance. This is not surprising since the means by which teaching performance is evaluated is currently in a substantial state of flux. While it cannot be stated with certainty, it seems reasonable to suggest that as academic deans gain additional experience using some of the newer components, such as "student evaluation" and "self-evaluation" of teaching performance, it may be expected that more uniformity of opinion will develop.

5. A slight increase has taken place since 1966 in the extent to which quality of teaching performance is considered a "major factor" in the evaluation of overall faculty performance in

liberal arts colleges. It cannot be determined from this study whether or not this slight increase represents a trend.

6. Substantial changes have occurred in the seven years since the Astin and Lee study with regard to the criteria used to evaluate overall faculty performance. Among criteria that have increased in use are "student advising" and "campus committee work." Criteria that have decreased in use in recent years include, among others, "research," "publication," "activity in professional societies," and "personal attributes." It appears that some of the more traditional criteria of faculty evaluation, which have been viewed as critically important for decades, have declined in importance. It cannot be determined from this study whether or not this represents a trend.

7. Substantial change has occurred in the seven years since the Astin and Lee study with regard to the types of information used in evaluating faculty teaching performance. Among types of information which have increased in use are "systematic student ratings," "committee evaluation," and "self-evaluation." A decline in use over the last seven years has taken place for "informal student opinions," "colleagues' opinions," "scholarly research and publication," "student examination performance," and "grade distributions." While an investigation into the reasons behind these changes is not within the scope of this study, it seems reasonable to suggest that a combination of student demands in the late 1960's for participation in academic decision-making, along with the financial bind that so many private colleges have experienced in recent years, has led to a change in emphasis in evaluation of the contribution to an academic institution of each staff member. These factors may have provided some of the impetus behind the changes in the types of information used to evaluate faculty teaching performance.

8. A substantial increase has occurred in the use of rating forms to evaluate the teaching performance of faculty members in liberal arts colleges. While fewer than one school in four reported use of rating forms in the Astin and Lee (1966) study, more than one half of the schools in the current investigation reported use of rating forms. The percentage of liberal arts colleges reporting that they have done research on the validity or usefulness of their rating forms has increased from 0.6 percent in the Astin and Lee study to 8.3 percent in the current study. It seems reasonable to suggest that the increased use of rating forms and research on these rating forms may be a reflection of an attempt by colleges to develop a more systematic and accurate means of evaluating faculty teaching performance. However, this suggestion cannot be stated with a high degree of certainty, since determination

of the reasons leading to increased use of rating forms and research on these rating forms is beyond the scope of this study.

9. The majority of academic deans of liberal arts colleges favor systematic student evaluation, although they oppose making the results public. They disagree with the view that classroom visitation by faculty colleagues is an invasion of academic privacy, but favor faculty self-evaluation as an important component in evaluation of performance.

10. Little or no difference exists between the level of importance assigned by liberal arts colleges to teaching behaviors evaluated for purposes of contract renewal as contrasted with the level of importance assigned to teaching behaviors evaluated for purposes of promotion in rank. From the data, it seems reasonable to suggest that one possible explanation is that certain teaching behaviors are regarded as important for good teaching, regardless of the purposes of evaluation. A quality teacher presumably exhibits many of these teaching behaviors in his teaching. Thus, whether for purposes of contract renewal or for promotion in rank, it seems likely that these same teaching behaviors are perceived as desirable when teaching performance is evaluated.

11. The differences that did exist between evaluation for purposes of contract renewal and evaluation for purposes of promotion in rank were related to use of written criteria. Written criteria in the evaluation of teaching performance for purposes of contract renewal was reportedly used by approximately 25 percent of the academic deans. A somewhat larger percentage, nearly 37 percent, of the academic deans reported use of written criteria when evaluating teaching performance for purposes of promotion in rank. While it cannot be stated with a high degree of certitude, it seems reasonable to suggest that contract renewal frequently occurs as a matter of course devoid of substantial evaluation of teaching performance. Promotion in rank, however, is often granted only after an elaborate procedure which includes the filing of a detailed application for promotion along with extensive supporting documentation. Thus, the more widespread use of written criteria for purposes of promotion in rank, as opposed to contract renewal, would seem to reflect the greater attention that is given to promotion in rank by many colleges.

RECOMMENDATIONS

A number of recommendations seem to be warranted by the results of this research investigation. Some of the recommendations relate to possible courses of action.

Possible courses of action. The following recommendations relate to possible courses of action and are a direct outgrowth of the findings of this research investigation:

1. There is a need for the development of a workable, objective, and systematic means of evaluating the teaching performance of faculty members. Considerable time, energy, and money could be saved if a prestigious panel made up of representatives of various interest groups including administrators, faculty, and students, funded by a substantial grant, was charged with the responsibility for developing a blueprint for faculty evaluation. The panel would have to be representative of colleges and universities of differing size, geographic location, and academic reputation. Subcommittees of the panel could be assigned different areas of investigation related to the evaluation of teaching performance of faculty members. Subcommittee reports, including specific recommendations for implementation of varying techniques, could then be combined in the overall panel report to the academic community. One of these subcommittees could address itself to systematic research on the evaluation process. This needs to be done in order that the value of appraisal, itself, be maximized. This blueprint for faculty evaluation could then be tailored by every college to meet its special needs.

2. A permanent committee on faculty evaluation should be appointed at every college and university. It should have as participants academic administrators, faculty, and students. The major function of this group should be the continual review of current evaluation policies and practices. In addition, the committee should be responsible for the adaptation to local conditions at their institution of the master plan which should be developed as outlined above by a nationwide panel.

3. Greater emphasis should be placed on self-evaluation as a major source of information to be used in appraising teaching performance. Because few faculty members are trained in objective self-evaluation techniques, it is most important that they be offered specific training on college campuses as well as in regional seminars and meetings. Faculty members can gain needed self-evaluation skills as well as a stronger appreciation for self-evaluation as a valuable appraisal technique.

4. Classroom visits for the purpose of obtaining information regarding faculty teaching performance should be encouraged. All teachers should be observed teaching at least once each semester by a two-person team consisting of a department colleague and the department chairman. Data gathered from classroom visits can

provide meaningful information for purposes of contract renewal and promotion in rank. Additional value could be derived from classroom observation through the use of post-observation meetings which would provide feedback to faculty members. The goal of these meetings would be the improvement of classroom instruction.

5. Annual faculty performance reviews should be required at all institutions. Department chairman and each faculty member should set mutually agreed upon goals which would be reviewed periodically and evaluated at the end of the academic year. Written goals, chairman evaluation reports and self-evaluation reports should be made available to the academic dean, department chairman and faculty member.

6. Systematized student evaluations should be undertaken to provide an additional source of information regarding teacher performance. To be meaningful, however, student evaluations must have administrative financial support as well as faculty directive support and encouragement. In addition, because few students are trained in the design of objective and meaningful evaluation questionnaires, it is important that they be given specific training either on their college campus or in regional seminars and meetings.

BIBLIOGRAPHY

Anthony, William, and John Lewis. Learning effectiveness: The measure of effective teaching. American Association of Collegiate Schools of Business Bulletin. IX, 1 (October, 1972).

Astin, Alexander, and Calvin B. T. Lee. Current Practices in the evaluation and training of college teachers. Improving College Teaching ed. Calvin B. T. Lee. Washington, D.C.: American Council on Education, 1967.

Bachman. Jerald. Faculty satisfaction and the dean's influence: An organizational study of twelve liberal arts colleges. Journal of Applied Psychology. LII, 1 (1969), 55-61.

Balyeat, Ralph E. Factors affecting the acquisition and retention of college faculty. U. S. Department of Health, Education and Welfare, Office of Education. December, 1968 (ER-10).

_____. Measuring teaching effectiveness. American Association of Collegiate Schools of Business Bulletin. VIII, 1 (October, 1971).

Bayley, D. H. Making college teaching a profession. Improving College and University Teaching. XV (1967), 115-119.

Biddle, Bruce J. The integration of teacher effectiveness research. Contemporary Research on Teacher Effectiveness, eds. Bruce J. Biddle and W. J. Ellena. New York: Holt, Rinehart and Winston, 1964.

Blackburn, Robert T. Changes in faculty life styles. Washington, D.C.: American Association for Higher Education. Research Report No. 1 (November, 1970).

_____. The professor's role in a changing society. ERIC Clearinghouse on Higher Education. Report No. 10 (June, 1971).

Brown, D. W. Teach or perish. Improving College and University Teaching. XV (1967), 108-110.

Bryan, R. C. Student ratings of teachers. Improving College and University Teaching. XVI (1968), 200-202.

_____ . Teacher's image is stubbornly stable. ERIC Clearinghouse on Higher Education. XL (1966), 459-461.

Bryant, P. T. By their fruits ye shall know them. The Journal of Higher Education. XXXVIII (1967), 326-330.

Byrnes, F. C., and J. X. Jamrich. Survey of policies and practices relating to improved instruction. Report to the meeting: Improvement of Instruction in Higher Education, American Association of Colleges for Teacher Education, 1962.

Carter, Allan M. University teaching and excellence. Improving College Teaching, ed. Calvin B. T. Lee. Washington, D.C.: American Council on Education, 1967.

Centra, John. Can teaching be evaluated? Paper read at the American Association for Higher Education Convestion, February, 1972.

Clark, Kenneth. Studies of faculty evaluation. Studies of College Faculty. Berkeley: Center for the Study of Higher Education, 1961.

Clark, Mary Jo, and Robert T. Blackburn. Assessment of faculty performance: Some correlates between self, colleagues, students, and administrators. Unpublished document.

Cohen, Arthur M., and Florence B. Brawer. Measuring faculty performance. Washington, D.C.: American Association of Junior Colleges. ERIC Clearinghouse for Junior Colleges, 1969.

Colgan, Fred E. Teaching effectiveness--a quality or quantity. American Association of Collegiate Schools of Business Bulletin. VIII, 1 (October, 1971).

Cook, J. Marvin, and Richard Neville. The faculty as teachers: A perspective on evaluation. Washington, D.C.: The George Washington University. ERIC Clearinghouse on Higher Education. Report 13 (September, 1971).

Crawford, D. L., and H. C. Bradshaw. Perception of characteristics of effective university teachers: A scaling analysis. Educational and Psychological Measurement. Winter, 1968.

Dixon, Wilfred J., and Frank J. Massey, Jr., Introduction to Statistical Analysis. New York: McGraw-Hill, 1957.

Dressel, Paul C. The Appraisal of Teaching in Large Universities, ed. W. J. McKeachie. Ann Arbor: University of Michigan, 1959.

_____. Evaluation of instruction. Journal of Farm Economics. XLIX (1967), 299.

Eble, Kenneth G. Professors As Teachers. San Francisco: Jossey-Bass, Inc., 1972.

_____. The recognition and evaluation of teaching. Washington, D.C.: Project to improve college teaching. American Association of University Professors and Association of American Colleges, 1970.

Ferguson, J. B. Job satisfaction and job performance within a university faculty. Unpublished doctoral dissertation, Cornell University, 1960.

Field, George R. Satisfaction and dissatisfactions of University of Wisconsin faculty members by campus location. Unpublished doctoral dissertation, University of Wisconsin, 1965.

Gaff, Jerry and Robert C. Wilson. New Teaching, New Learning, ed. G. Kerry Smith. Washington: American Association for Higher Education, Jossey-Bass, Inc., 1971.

Gage, N. L. The appraisal of college teaching. Journal of Higher Education, XXXII (1961), 17-22.

Goforth, Gene Bales. Desirable characteristics of college teachers as received by presidents and deans of selected liberal arts colleges. Unpublished doctoral dissertation, Indiana University 1966.

Gray, C. E. The teaching model and evaluation of teaching performance. Journal of Higher Education. XL (1969), 636-642.

Gustad, John W. Policies and practices in faculty evaluation. Educational Record. July, 1961.

————. Evaluation of teaching performance. Improving College Teaching, ed. Calvin B. T. Lee. Washington, D.C.: American Council on Education, 1967.

Harvey, J. N., and D. G. Barker. Student evaluation of teaching effectiveness. Improving College and University Teaching. XVIII (1970), 275-278.

Hildebrand, M., and R. C. Wilson. Effective University Teaching and Its Evaluation. Berkeley: Center for Research and Development in Higher Education, 1970.

Hill, Winston. Some organizational correlates of sanctions perceived by professors to be available to their department chairmen: A study in power. Unpublished doctoral dissertation, University of Washington, 1965.

Hind, Robert Renton, Jr. Evaluation and authority in a university faculty. Unpublished doctoral dissertation, Stanford University, 1969.

Hodgkinson, Harold. Assessment and reward systems. New Teaching, New Learning, ed. G. Kerry Smith. Washington: American Association for Higher Education, Jossey-Bass, Inc., 1971.

Howe, Harold, II. Less teaching, more conversation. Improving College Teaching, ed. Calvin B. T. Lee. Washington, D.C.: American Council on Education, 1967.

Hoyt, Donald D. Instructional effectiveness: I. Measurement of effectiveness. Kansas State University, Office of Educational Research. Research Report 6 (November, 1968).

Hunter, J. O. Faculty evaluations as a liberal persuasion. Improving College and University Teaching. XVII (1969), 90-92.

Hussain, K. R., and Robert Legstamper. Survey of criteria of teaching effectiveness at New Mexico State University. Las Cruces: New Mexico State University, June, 1968.

Isaacson, R. L., and others. Correlation of teacher personality variables and student ratings. Journal of Educational Psychology. LIV (1963), 110-117.

Karman, T. A. Faculty evaluation. Liberal Education. LV (1969), 539-544.

Kerlinger, F. N. Student evaluation of university professors. School and Society. XCIX (October, 1971), 353-356.

Kirchner, R. P. A central factor in teacher evaluation by students. Unpublished research paper, University of Kentucky, College of Education, 1969.

Langden, T. D. F. Student Assessment of teaching effectiveness. Improving College and University Teaching. XIV (1966), 22-25.

Luthans, Frederick. The faculty promotion process and analysis of the management of large state universities. University of Iowa, College of Business Administration, Bureau of Business and Economic Research, 1967.

McKeachie, W. J. Research in teaching. Improving College Teaching ed. Calvin B. T. Lee. Washington, D.C.: American Council on Education, 1967.

———. Student ratings of faculty. AAUP Bulletin. LV (1969), 439-447.

———. Yi-Guang Lin, and William Man. Student ratings of teacher effectiveness: Validity studies. American Educational Research Journal, VIII, 3 (May, 1971), 444.

Mayhew, L. B. A tissue committee for teachers. Improving College and University Teaching. XV (1967).

Megaw, Neill. The dynamics of evaluation. Improving College Teaching, ed. Calvin B. T. Lee. Washington, D.C.: American Council on Education, 1967.

Miller, Richard C. Evaluating Faculty Performance. San Francisco: Jossey-Bass, Inc., 1972.

Mitzel, H. E. Teacher effectiveness. Encyclopedia of Educational Research. New York: MacMillan Co., 1960.

Morton, R. K. Evaluating college teaching. Improving College and University Teaching. IX (1961), 122-123.

Musella, D., and R. Rusch. Student opinion on college teaching. Improving College and University Teaching. XVI (1968), 137-140.

Neeley, Melvin. A teacher's view of teacher evaluation. Improving College and University Teaching. XVI (1968), 207-209.

Oxmon, H. Publications and teaching. Improving College and University Teaching. XV (1967), 106-107.

Perry, R. R. Criteria of effective teaching in an institution of higher education. Ohio: University of Toledo, Office of Institutional Research, 1969, 8-24.

Pogue, F. G., Jr. Students' ratings of the ideal teacher. Improving College and University Teaching. XV (1967), 133-136.

Priest, B. J. Classrooms: Castles or learning laboratories. Improving College Teaching, ed. Calvin B. T. Lee. Washington, D.C.: American Council on Education, 1967.

Rayder, N. F. College student ratings of instructors. The Journal of Experimental Education. XXXVIII (1968), 76-81.

Renner, R. R. A successful rating scale. Improving College and University Teaching. XV (1967), 12-14.

Robinson, Lora H. Improving college teaching through faculty selection and evaluation: A review. Currents '70. ERIC Clearinghouse on Higher Education. No. 2 (July, 1970).

Rodin, Miriam, and Burton Rodin. Student evaluations of teachers Science. CLXXVII (September 29, 1972).

Rothwell, C.E. The importance of teaching--A memorandum to the new college teacher. Report of the Committee on Under-graduate Teaching. New Haven, Connecticut: Hazen Foundation, 1968.

Rovin, S. (ed.). Evaluation of teaching and teachers. Proceedings of the Faculty Conference, University of Kentucky, College of Dentistry, 1967.

Samaconis, B. Ratings by students. Improving College and University Teaching. XV (1967), 11.

Schwartz, R.   Student power-In response to the questions.
Report to meeting: The future academic community; Con-
tinuity and change. American Council on Education Annual
Meeting, 1968.

Schmeller,   Kurt.   One-page memorandum to Queensboro
Community College Faculty, April, 1972.

Sherman, Barbara R. Some characteristics of a small college
faculty. Unpublished report. The University of Michigan,
Center for the Study of Higher Education, 1969.

Shoben, Edward Joseph, Jr. Gimmicks and concepts in the assessment of teaching. Improving College Teaching, ed. Calvin
B. T. Lee. Washington, D.C.: American Council on Education,
1967.

Simpson, R. H., and J. M. Seidman. Use of teacher self-eval-
uative tools for the improvement of instruction. Report to
the meeting: Improvement of Instruction in Higher Education,
American Association of Colleges for Teacher Education,
1962.

Slobin, D. Y., and O. G. Nichols. Student ratings of teaching
Improving College and University Teaching. XVII (1969),
244-248.

Smart, R. C. The evaluation of teaching performance from the
point   of   view   of   the   teaching profession. American
Psychological Association Meeting, Chicago, 1965.

Stewart, C. T., and L. F. Maldass. Estimates of achievement and
ratings of instructors. Journal of Educational Research,
LIX (1966), 347-350.

Swanson, Carol, and Charles Weaver. Faculty appraisal: Current
Practices in schools of business. Journal of Business
Education. XLVII (March, 1972).

Theophilus, N. Professional attitudes toward their work at the
University of Michigan. Unpublished doctoral dissertation,
University of Michigan, 1967.

Tyler, Ralph W. The evaluation of teaching. Preparing College teachers, eds. A. D. Albright and John B. Burrows. Lexington, Kentucky: University of Kentucky and Atlanta, Georgia: Southern Regional Education Board, 1959.

Werdell, Philip. Course and Teacher Evaluation. 2d ed. Washington, D.C.: U. S. National Student Association, 1967.

Winthrop, H. Worth of a colleague. Improving College and University Teaching. XIV (1966), 262-267.

APPENDIX

Part I

EVALUATION OF OVERALL FACULTY PERFORMANCE

A. Instructions:

What factors are principally considered in evaluating a faculty member for promotion in rank, salary increase or tenure? Please indicate the importance of each factor by placing a check mark (✓) in the appropriate column after each factor. (Please check one answer in each row.)

IBM Code ▼ Factors	(1) Major Factor	(2) Minor Factor	(3) Not A Factor	(4) Not Applicable
1. Classroom teaching				
2. Supervision of graduate study				
3. Supervision of honors program				
4. Research				
5. Publication				
6. Public service				
7. Consultation (government, business)				
8. Activity in professional societies				
9. Student advising				
10. Campus committee work				
11. Length of service in rank				
12. Competing job offers				
13. Personal attributes				
14. Other (specify)				

EVALUATION OF TEACHING PERFORMANCE

B. Instructions:

Please indicate the frequency with which each of the following types of information is used in your college in evaluating a faculty member's <u>teaching performance.</u> (Please check one answer in each row.)

Types of Information	(1) Always Used	(2) Usually Used	(3) Seldom Used	(4) Never Used
15. Systematic student ratings				
16. Informal student opinions				
17. Classroom visits				
18. Colleagues' opinions				
19. Scholarly research and publication				
20. Student examination performance				
21. Chairman evaluation				
22. Dean evaluation				
23. Course syllabi and examinations				
24. Long term follow-up of students				
25. Enrollment in elective courses				
26. Alumni opinions				
27. Committee evaluation				
28. Grade distributions				
29. Self evaluation or report				
30. Other				

METHODS USED TO LEARN ABOUT TEACHING PERFORMANCE

C.
31. Do you routinely employ any special rating forms or other instruments in collecting data on teaching competence? Please check the appropriate answer.   Yes_____No_____
(If yes, please attach copies of these instruments.)

IBM
Code

Part II

32. Has your institution developed research concerning the validity or usefulness of these instruments? Please check the appropriate answer.   Yes _____ No _____

Personal Judgment Questions

D. **Instructions:**
    Your personal judgment is wanted rather than a report of the on-going policies and practices in your college. Please indicate your reaction to each of the following statements by placing a check mark (✓) next to the responses that most closely reflect your personal judgment.

	Strongly Agree ◄————————————————————►	Strongly Disagree

33. The results of systematic student evaluation of a faculty member's teaching performance indicate more about a teacher's popularity than about his teaching performance.   _____ 1 _____ 2 _____ 3 _____ 4

34. The results of systematic student evaluation of a faculty member's teaching performance should be made public.   _____ 1 _____ 2 _____ 3 _____ 4

35. Systematic and planned classroom visitation by faculty colleagues for the purpose of evaluating a faculty member's teaching performance is an invasion of academic privacy.   _____ 1 _____ 2 _____ 3 _____ 4

36. Results of an institutionalized, uniform approach to faculty self-evaluation should be one of the important components in evaluation of faculty teaching performance.   _____ 1 _____ 2 _____ 3 _____ 4

37. The academic personnel policies and practices used to evaluate a faculty member's teaching performance are well known by most members of the faculty.   _____ 1 _____ 2 _____ 3 _____ 4

38. Academic personnel decisions made in liberal arts colleges are based primarily on objective information (that is, information that is rational, impersonal and unprejudiced).   _____ 1 _____ 2 _____ 3 _____ 4

E. Please indicate the importance that you personally give to each of the following components that have been proposed for use in the evaluation of a faculty member's teaching performance by numbering them in rank order.

39. _____ student evaluation of teaching performance
40. _____ faculty colleague evaluation of teaching performance
41. _____ self-evaluation of teaching performance
42. _____ chairman evaluation of teaching performance

> The following questions concern the policies and practices employed in evaluating teaching performance specifically for contract renewal and for promotion in rank decisions.

Present Level of Satisfaction with Policies and Practices

F. **Instructions:**
    Please indicate the level of satisfaction you feel with policies and practices currently used to evaluate classroom teaching performance. Indicate your views separately for contract renewal and promotion in rank decisions. Place a check mark (✓) next to the answer for contract renewal and again for promotion in rank which most closely reflects your personal feelings.

Which of the following answers do you believe most closely represent the <u>view of most of the faculty</u> in connection with current evaluation policies and practices:

43. Contract   44. Promotion
    Renewal   In Rank

(1)_____   (1) _____   Satisfied with <u>all</u> policies and practices
(2)_____   (2) _____   Satisfied with <u>most</u> policies and practices
(3)_____   (3) _____   Satisfied with <u>few</u> policies and practices
(4)_____   (4) _____   Satisfied with <u>none</u> of the policies and practices

Which of the following answers most closely represents your own view in connection with current evaluation policies and practices:

45. Contract   46. Promotion
    Renewal   In Rank

(1)_____   (1) _____   Satisfied with <u>all</u> policies and practices
(2)_____   (2) _____   Satisfied with <u>most</u> policies and practices
(3)_____   (3) _____   Satisfied with <u>few</u> policies and practices
(4)_____   (4) _____   Satisfied with <u>none</u> of the policies and practices

G. Does your college apply a check list of written criteria in measuring and evaluating teaching performance of faculty members?

47. For Contract Renewal   48. For Promotion in Rank
_____Yes _____ No   _____Yes _____ No

Importance of Specific Teaching Behaviors

H. Instructions:
Please rate the level of importance that your college assigns to each of the following teaching behaviors for the purpose of evaluating teaching performance of faculty members. Place a check mark (✓) at the appropriate response level for both contract renewal and promotion in rank.

IBM Code / Teaching Behaviors	Contract Renewal				IBM Code	Promotion in Rank			
	Most Important		Least Important			Most Important		Least Important	
	1	2	3	4		1	2	3	4
49. Is well prepared for class					59.				
50. Demonstrates comprehensive subject knowledge					60.				
51. Motivates students to do their best					61.				
52. Encourages intelligent independent thought by students					62.				
53.* Treats students with respect					63.				
54. Discusses points of view other than his own					64.				
55. Is dynamic and energetic person					65.				
56. Seems to enjoy teaching					66.				
57. Communicates effectively to the level of his students					67.				
58. Is fair and reasonable to students in grading procedures					68.				

College Data: (Please check the appropriate answer for your college)
69. Number of <u>full-time</u> faculty: (1)__ 50 or less   (2)__ 51-100   (3)_____ 101-150   (4)__151 or more
70. Average freshman college boards: (1)__ 475 or less   (2)__476-550   (3)__ 551-625   (4)__ 626 or more

Comments: Your comments are invited. Please use reverse side of this page.